The Father's Heart

Meet the Real Abba Father

Book One

10 Spiritual Exercises
to Heal from the Wounds of the Heart

Terry A. Modica

En Route Books and Media, LLC
Saint Louis, MO

ENROUTE
Make the time

En Route Books and Media, LLC
5705 Rhodes Avenue
St. Louis, MO 63109

Cover credit: Terry A. Modica

Copyright © 2024 Terry A. Modica

ISBN-13: 979-8-88870-208-6 and 979-8-88870-209-3
Library of Congress Control Number: 2024943300

No part of this book may be reproduced, stored in a retrieval system, or transmitted in any form, or by any means, electronic, mechanical, photocopying, or otherwise, without the prior written permission of the author.

Dedication

This book is in your hands because of some special people in my life. First, I would like to dedicate this book to my spiritual mentor, Irene Huber, who introduced me to God the Father during an inner healing session. Although Irene long ago passed from this Earth, she is so deeply embedded in the Father's heart now that I'm sure her prayers have helped get this book finished and delivered to you.

Of course, I also thank my parents, Pam and Don Repsher, for showing me what real parental love is despite their imperfections. My dad read an early version of this book (all three parts of it) before he passed away in 2020.

With great appreciation, I also dedicate this book to the people who shared their stories so that I could better illustrate points I make.

Most of all, I dedicate this book to my husband, Ralph, who unexpectedly passed away in February of 2024. He was my cheerleader throughout the years that I worked on this book. He was my biggest fan. And a lot of what I learned about God's fatherhood came from my observations of how he fathered our children, David and Tammy. Over the 48 years of our marriage, we had many discussions about fatherhood; he taught me much about what I had missed during my childhood. As you use this book, send a thank-you to him on the wings of your guardian angel. Ralph will smile, forward your thank-you to God, and tell you, "When you were baptized, God the Father looked at you and said, 'You are my beloved child; I am very pleased with you.'" Ralph said that to a lot of people when he lived on Earth.

Table of Contents

Foreword by Bear Woznick v

Introduction: What are you seeking? 1

1 Tears for Abba 7

2 Healing Your Image of God's Fatherhood 25

3 The Name of Abba, Like No Other Name 47

4 Words That Make a Difference 71

5 The Safest Father in the World 89

6 The Father Heals Us of Fear 113

7 When Doubts Tell Us God Doesn't Care 131

8 Dealing with Disappointment 149

9 The Discipline of Abba-Father 173

10 Abba's Hidden Love in Our Confusion 189

Foreword

"Meet the Real Abba Father"–in this time, now more than ever, we need to know who our heavenly Father really is; not just to know about Him but to know Him.

I have walked the streets of Jerusalem and heard the sweet sound of a little child calling out to their father in excitement: "Abba! Abba!" It is a word that communicates endearment and respect for the father.

Very few people make it through to adulthood without a "father wound," to some degree or other, that is brought on by a distant or demanding or angry father or just a good man trying to be a good Dad but failing to live up to all that the child really needs. It is a wound from that old serpent, Satan himself, whom Jesus said was also a father–the "father of lies"–and we cannot imagine calling God "Dad." We need to know and believe the truth about our heavenly Father.

God has good intentions for us and is working to bring about our healing if we will only let Him. "'For I know the plans I have for you,' declares the Lord, 'plans to prosper you and not to harm you, plans to give you hope and a future. You will seek me and find me when you seek me with all your heart'" (Jeremiah 29:11, 13 NIV). We can push Him away and reject Him. But He is always moving towards us in love. Seek Him and seek to know Him as He really is.

We may feel that God the Father is distant or judgmental, unapproachable, stern and even a bit scary. Just to say the first two words of the prayer that Jesus taught us–"Our Father"–seems to place a wall between us and God, even though His Word teaches us that "God is Love." For myself, in the past and even now, when I find myself falling into that place of feeling like God is distant or uncaring or stern, I have learned to open my heart to Him by calling Him "Abba Father" or, to use our Hawaiian word for father, "Makua." It reminds me of the love he has for me and how approachable He is to me as His child.

Terry Modica shares with you, in her "Father's Heart" series, springs of joy that will open and heal your heart as you meet and grow to know the "Real Abba Father."

Bear Woznick
EWTN TV & Radio Host
World Champ Surfer
Author of "12 Rules For Manliness - Where Have All the Cowboys Gone"

Introduction

What are you seeking?

What is it that you're seeking from God? Do you know that, if it's good and God doesn't have a better plan, you already have what you seek? It often takes time for it to be revealed and understood, but God has already granted it.

Most of us don't have the level of faith that makes waiting for God's help a joyful, peaceful time. That's because we don't fully trust God.

When you've cried over unanswered prayers, who did you blame? For most of my life, I blamed myself. God could not possibly be at fault. He was perfect. He was all-good. He loved me unconditionally. So, I worked hard at my spiritual growth. I wanted to have faith that was at least the size of a tiny mustard seed. Apparently, according to Jesus, only a little bit of faith is enough to move mountains. "Nothing would be impossible for you," he said (see Matthew 17:20). And apparently my faith was smaller than that.

During my young adult years, after a major conversion experience in which I recommitted myself to Christ, people told me about miracles they received. However, when I prayed for miracles, nothing happened. "It must be me," I thought. "Something's wrong with my faith." I was so sure of this that when others came together to pray for anything amazing, I left the room afraid that my lack of faith would somehow prevent them from receiving what they asked for from God.

Determined to find my way into the mustard seed-size faith that can move mountains, I immersed myself in scripture studies, prayer groups, parish events, and anything else that seemed faith-building. Many good fruits came from this daily effort, including a few answered prayers, but not enough. Faith had to be better than this!

Deep down, when we try and try but fail to have the kind of faith that gets results from our prayer requests, we don't really blame ourselves. We blame God. He is, after all, way more powerful than we are. He can make miracles happen despite our smaller-than-mustard-seed faith.

This raises terrible questions, such as: Has God abandoned me? Is he ignoring me? Does he care about others more than he cares about me? We ask because we *feel* abandoned, ignored, and uncared for, and we don't want to believe that God would do that to us.

One day as I cried because I felt ignored by God, an image of a cardboard box came to mind. It wasn't a very big box—about the size of a microwave oven. I wondered what might be in it.

"You have put Me in a box," I heard in my own inner voice, but I knew it was not my voice. "You have been limiting Me. You see Me as less than *I Am*. Open the box and let Me out."

Gladly! I visualized the lid of the box opening up, and I imagined God escaping from it and expanding larger and larger until he filled the universe.

This began a lifelong quest to unpack who God really is and what he is really like. God as a loving, doting, perfect Father who desires more than we do for our prayers to be answered. God as the infinite, unlimited, all-powerful Father who wants to use his mightiness for our benefit. God as the Father who solves our problems and lifts us up above them.

In the parishes where I've worked in adult faith formation and through Good News Ministries (the Catholic faith-building ministry that my husband, Ralph, and I founded in 1995), I've made it my goal to help people meet the real Father. Everywhere, I see the need for spiritual healing that comes from perceiving God as less than he is.

We limit the size of our faith by projecting onto God the imperfections that we've witnessed in the humans around us. However, because no one—not even the best of parents—can be God for us, we yearn to be fathered by him, and at the same time we have a hard time seeing him as more than what we have witnessed in others.

Furthermore, fatherhood has been severely undermined in society. And this has diluted people's understanding of the True God. The world today desperately needs to be converted to Christ, but our power as Christians to change the world for Christ is weakened by our own distrust in God the Father.

Therefore, I prepared a set of three workbooks on *The Father's Heart*, all to help you experience the wonderfulness of the True Father so that your faith can be set free to reach its full potential:

1. *Meet the Real Abba Father*
2. *Love that Heals Your Deepest Longing*
3. *The Victory of God's Fatherhood*

Each one of these, used in this order, are inspirational guides to healing that will enable you to experience God the Father as he truly is. The books use scriptures, true life stories, and theological reflection. We'll identify and overcome the most common misconceptions that interfere with faith in God.

This series is filled with true stories from my own personal journey and the experiences of others. While writing the first draft, I shared each chapter with volunteers who had signed up to give feedback. Many of them gave me their personal stories to include in the final version.

Although each situation is unique, the feelings, blessings, and problems they generate are universal. It's my hope that the stories will assure you that you are not alone in your pain. This realization is often the beginning of healing. Storytelling helps make the truth sink deeper into our hearts where real change occurs.

To be effective, we need to be honest. Some people have expressed discomfort over the frankness of my personal stories. "Are you being hurtful to your parents?" they wondered. Rest assured that my parents read this book during its development, and my dad (who has since passed away) helped me to remember some of the details more accurately. They were/are both happy that this book will help others get to know the deep love of God the Father more fully.

There are writing exercises in each chapter to empower you to travel deeper and deeper into the Father's heart. Each chapter will generate new insights that will forever change how you view God as your True Father.

My friendship with the Father deepened as I wrote this book. I pray that yours will, too—to astounding new heights of joy and depths of intimacy and an ever-widening trust in the Father's love for you.

In God's smile,
Terry Modica

For this reason I kneel before the Father, from whom every family in heaven and on earth derives its name. I pray that out of his glorious riches he may strengthen you with power through his Spirit in your inner being, so that Christ may dwell in your hearts through faith. And I pray that you, being rooted and established in love, may have power, together with all the Lord's holy people, to grasp how wide and long and high and deep is the love of Christ, and to know this love that surpasses knowledge—that you may be filled to the measure of all the fullness of God. (Ephesians 3:14-19 NIV)

1

Tears for Abba

Do you remember crying because your daddy wasn't there for you when you needed him? Or your mama? You've been carrying around a father-wound and a mother-wound that God wants to heal. Let me introduce you to Abba-Daddy Who Wipes Away Your Tears.

I pray that you, being rooted and established in love, may have power, together with all the Lord's holy people, to grasp how wide and long and high and deep is the love of Christ, and to know this love that surpasses knowledge—that you may be filled to the measure of all the fullness of God. (Ephesians 3:17b-19 NIV)

My earliest memory is a scene in the kitchen. From my seat in the baby's high chair, I see Mommy washing dishes. Daddy comes into the room demanding that she serve him a bowl of ice cream (he always called it "wife-dipped ice cream" because he wanted her to serve him). I'm not old enough to understand why the tone of his voice disturbs me nor why Mommy gets upset. What I do remember—and rather vividly—is a ball of ice cream flying across the room, thrust from her spoon toward my father.

Although loud fighting was not common in my childhood home, their quarrel that day became permanently etched in my psyche. Sixty-plus years later, I still tense up when I witness people argue loudly with each other. I want to intervene. I want to bring peace. And at the same time, I feel completely incapable of making a difference because deep inside I'm still that two-year-old surprised by the scoop of ice cream flying across the room.

The next life-changing event that I remember occurred four years later. At six years old, a child's brain develops an ability to understand her environment and reason out what's good, what's bad, and what should be but is not. At six years old, I came to a devastating conclusion: My daddy was not the warm, friendly, understanding, compassionate listener that I needed him to be. Whatever triggered this realization is lost in the past, but I remember grieving deeply and making the decision, which held for the rest of my life, that I would never again call him "Daddy." The name didn't fit. "Dad" was more acceptable. It felt less intimate. It acknowledged his fatherhood while representing the sad lack of father-daughter closeness.

My dad was basically a good father. His flaws tell only part of the story. He loved his wife and children dearly, and I knew it. He was not abusive. He made it a priority to attend my school events. He figured out ways for the family to have fun together, including awesome vacations, despite being poor. He taught us how to have a balanced life. And, most importantly, with my mother he introduced me to Christ and taught me to pray.

The problem was: I had discovered that my father was not *The Father*.

Seeking the Father

Every person is created by God to know him, to love him, to serve him in this world, and to be happy with him forever in Heaven. Saint Paul wrote, "*Praise be to the God and Father of our Lord Jesus Christ, who has blessed us in the heavenly realms with every spiritual blessing in Christ.* **For he chose us in him before the creation of the world** *to be holy and blameless in his sight*" (Ephesians 1:3-4 NIV; emphasis mine).

You and I were created to be like our Divine Father; we were made in his image (Genesis 1:26). Therefore, since the moment of our entrance into this unholy world, we instinctively have been seeking the Perfect Father who made us. However, until we learn how to have a close, intimate relationship with God as our Father, we will keep looking for him in his closest representatives: Fathers, mothers, aunts and uncles, foster parents, grandparents, teachers, best friends, clergy, etc.

In my forty-plus years of ministry, I've encountered many who are seeking the Perfect Father in the people around them without consciously realizing that this is why they continually feel disappointed and hurt. Many of us end up in divorces and other broken relationships because of this. It's also why ministers and priests disappoint us: We look to them for the best examples of God's Fatherhood, but they are all imperfect. Sadly, their failure to be the God that we want them to be causes indignation and outrage, a reduction in donations to the Church, separation from the parish, and—all too often—separation from the very God we're seeking.

No one can love us the way God loves us. Everyone whom we rely on for the love and care and support we need are imperfect representatives of God the Father.

Throughout my childhood, I expected my daddy to be God. Of course, I didn't realize this because I thought I had already found God. Jesus has been my Savior and a close companion for as long as I can remember. When I was a child, having a close relationship with Jesus seemed to be enough. In reality, it was not.

It would take another twenty years before I came to know God as my Father. Meanwhile, my dad, like all human fathers, continued to fail to be the Father for whom I deeply longed. Although he did a lot of things right, every imperfection stood out as a big reminder that he failed to be what I wished him to be. My mother wasn't perfect either, and her shortcomings contributed to my false images of God. So did the third grade teacher who embarrassed me in front of the class. And, after I became an adult, the policeman who gave me a speeding ticket instead of letting me go with just a warning. (And so forth with every human authority figure.)

Created to be loved

Father God gave us life and created us to be loved. Ever since he created the Earth, he's been looking forward to having a close, loving relationship with you. You are God's handiwork (see Ephesians 2:10). Deep in the soul of every child is an awareness that his or her life comes from God *"the Creator of the heavens, who stretches them out, who spreads out the earth with all that springs from it, who gives breath to its people, and life to those who walk on it"* (Isaiah 42:5 NIV).

Every child instinctively knows that God exists and that he is the source of love and that he is perfect. Want proof of this? Consider how strong is the impulse to expect perfection from humans. We have all been seeking him (although unconsciously) in the people around us since our babyhood—especially in those who were our first representatives of his Fatherhood.

God created us for love. Psychologists have long recognized that the need to be loved is the strongest of psychological needs. When we feel unloved, we are profoundly sad, emotionally hungry, and shaken to the core. It can lead to despair, and it's a very short walk between despair and suicide.

God designed into the very fabric of our being a natural yearning to receive *his* love, to be embraced securely by *his* caring compassion, so that we cling to him all the way into eternity. We were born with a divine knowledge of what love is supposed to feel like, what it's supposed to look like, and how it's supposed to be shared.

Have you ever watched a small child follow his or her parent? One day during weekday Mass, God taught me about his Fatherhood as I watched a young mother and her two pre-school sons. The older boy was getting too rambunctious, so she stood up to take him outside. She signaled the younger one to stay in his seat. As she walked toward the door, he watched her steadily. Nothing else mattered. His instinct was to jump up and run after her, but he fought it. Up he stood and then obediently sat down. Then up again when his mom opened the door to leave. He started to move toward her but then returned to his seat. It became especially hard for him when she disappeared from view, and finally he gave in to his inner yearning and ran after her.

In the animal world, this is called "imprinting." The first creature that a freshly hatched duckling sees becomes its mother, which it dutifully follows everywhere even if the mother waddles across a busy street in front of oncoming traffic. Fortunately, human parents are a lot smarter than ducks.

When you and I were little, we had the same instinct to follow our parents. It's a built-in survival mechanism. It's the primal example of trust. Jesus used this as an example of how we adults should trust Father God. He said in effect: *"Unless you become like little children, you will never be able to follow your Father to Heaven"* (adapted from Matthew 18:3).

However, since our human parents were not perfect—because they were not God—following them sometimes led us smack into the oncoming traffic of worldly ideas, misunderstandings, and arguments that caused ice cream to fly. And sometimes it crashed us into their anger, their unhealed wounds, and, for some readers, their deliberate abuses.

We all need healing

Take a few minutes to think of some of the ways that the imperfections of your parents (or guardians) and other authority figures have caused you to suffer. Do you remember crying because your daddy wasn't there for you when you needed him? Or your mama? Did a father-figure punish you when you didn't deserve it (or maybe you did deserve it but at the time you felt innocent)? Did a parent fail to come see you at a school event? Were both your parents away at work when you needed a hug after a bad day at school? Was your father separated from you by divorce or death or long travels for his job? Was an important person in your life too drunk to notice your needs? Or too busy?

Pause to bring these hurts to mind. Father God wants to heal them!

This exercise of remembering is not meant to ignore what was good about these people. We're setting the stage for a closer relationship with God the Ultimate Parent. We're not fault-finding; we're seeking God. We need to recall the imperfections of humans because this is how we overcome our false images of the Divine Father. This is how we open ourselves to the healing love of the only parent who is perfect. Even the best of parents unintentionally hurt their children because of human limitations and because of how they, too, were treated by their own imperfect parents.

> (1) Next, think about the examples of insufficient love that you learned by witnessing the imperfections of others. Do you have a spouse who was unfaithful to you? Or a boss who never deals with problems in the company? Or parents who changed after you became an adult, as we see in Debbie's story? She says:
>> "All my childhood memories are wonderful of my parents. Sure, we were disciplined, and at times I felt things were unfair, especially when I was a teenager, but for the most part I know that all the discipline was for my own good. Unfortunately, in their last years, my parents seemed to be fighting

verbally with one another. What is so hard for me is wondering, because I grew up thinking they were the best parents and in love with each other, how could they be so unkind to one another in their last years? My heart is broken not seeing them love each other openly on a daily basis."

(2) Listen to how that translates into her relationship with God:

"I want to see God Our Father as the one I call on throughout the day (a hard habit for me to form). My question is: How do we become more childlike, trusting God in our daily life?"

(3) Who has taught you to be distrustful? Cynical? Guarded? Charmaine says:

"It is so difficult for me to totally trust God, to surrender all to him. I keep trying to fix me but to no avail. You see, when as a child, my siblings called me bad names and I cannot remember ever being defended by either parent."

(4) Who has taught you to be jealous? Do you believe that God favors others more than you? That he answers the prayers of others while saying "no" to you? Listen to Tonia's story:

"I continually remember the time during my senior year of high school that I wanted to become a dental assistant. At the time, our city did not offer classes and I would have to go to a city that was quite a distance. My parents refused my request. However, my oldest sister, who was the perfect daughter at the top of her high school and college graduating classes, was never refused when she asked to go away just as far. I felt like the child who is always walking in her shadow but never good enough!"

(5) Who has rejected you and made you fear abandonment? Kay lived in a loving home, and yet:

"There was always an emotional distancing from my Dad. He and my Mom shared an amazing love for each other that I, as their only child, never really felt a part of. I felt protected, I felt loved, but I also felt like the "third wheel." As a result, while I believed in God the Father, he was a distant supervisor of my life and not at all someone I would go to for comfort and solace. Mom and Dad had frequent arguments that scared me because I feared abandonment. These arguments were always followed by long periods of silence. My life, up until my Dad died, was colored by issues of abandonment, rejection, fear of his anger, lack of warmth, criticism, and other concerns, all of which shaped my thinking and beliefs about God the Father.

"When my Dad died, I was given the opportunity to care for my Mother who was in the late stages of Alzheimer's. I developed a whole new perspective of my Dad and a great deal of respect for the man that he was. That perspective allowed me to develop a different relationship with God the Father and a great love for the comfort and guidance he offers for me and all his children."

(6) Who made you feel "not good enough"? Note: There is another side of God that we must also consider. Although we refer to him in manly terms, God is not limited to manly traits. He is both a Father and a Mother to us. He has the nurturing qualities of motherhood as much as he has the protective qualities of fatherhood. What is your ideal image of the perfect mother? God is the source of that. He has given us the perfect example of motherhood in the flesh in the Mother of Jesus. And yet, as Maureen's story tells us, we feel like we're missing out on the motherly love of God:

"I know my mother loved me, but I don't remember her being loving toward me. I only remember her being judgmental and distant, unlike my father. I have no trouble relating to Abba-Father. He is my everything, just as in my childhood my father was kind and self-effacing. But even at the ripe old age of 72, I struggle with mother issues."

(7) And what about other authority figures? Priests and ministers are charged with a very special responsibility of representing God. They are supposed to be our spiritual fathers. Mary says:

"I personally have had an awakening in my relationship with priests as representations of God. Growing up I was told they were 'God on Earth for us' and so I have had more than a few disappointments finding out they were really 'only human'."

The key to knowing the Father's Heart

Recalling the sources of our poor images of Father God is key to getting to know him as he really is. However, part of the healing process is to also remember how our parents (and others in positions of authority) revealed the truth about God. For example, my dad represented God's Fatherhood very well in his protection of the family. I grew up feeling the love that inspired his protectiveness. A favorite memory comes from the time when Ralph and I were dating. We were high school sweethearts. Ralph's father was very suspicious of me due to his own protectiveness.

When Ralph drove me home from our dates, we usually talked for hours parked in the driveway. When my family vacated the living room by going to bed, Ralph and I brought our discussion (and smooching) indoors.

Around 10:00 one night, while Ralph and I cuddled on the couch, deep in conversation, the phone rang. My parents had just gone to bed. Dad answered the phone. Ralph's father was calling to find out if Ralph was with me. And then he insisted, quite irately, that Ralph should be sent home immediately.

What happened next made me feel very good about my dad. He defended Ralph! He protected our right to be together. He made a difference by standing up for us.

Any scary experience during childhood can become a misconception about God. And the reverse is true: The ways we felt protected when we were young can become trust in God.

My dad counseled a man who was mentally unstable. He tried to help him spiritually while a psychiatrist dealt with his problems psychologically and medically. Unfortunately, this man became violent and attacked his psychiatrist, beating him into a veritable human vegetable with a hammer to his skull. While he was still on the loose, the police informed my dad that he might come after him next. So, my dad sent me and my sister and brother to the house across the street.

We watched from a window as police cars patrolled the area. From the vantage point of safety, the situation seemed like an adventure, like I was living out a cop show on television.

Years later, when faced with a challenge that involves taking risks, I have enough trust in God to feel exhilarated by the adventure. Certainly, there is some degree of worrying about what's going to happen, but if I've sensed the Father's calling or go-ahead in the troublesome situation, I trust that he is protecting me. I trust that he has a plan that's so good, even if things go wrong they will turn out to be used for good (as Romans 8:28 promises).

Because I grew up feeling protected by my parents, when I've needed God's protection, I have felt it. Think now about your own father, mother, and other significant parental influences. In what ways did they portray or represent God's wonderfulness? Laura shares this:

"I grew up with a dad that expected perfection. If he said jump, you asked how high on the way up. If you brought home an "A" from school, why not an "A+"? But he also was the one who told you that you sang the best in your class, and I believed it! As I have grown I have realized he just wanted the best for me."

It's good to think about what our parents did right more often than you think about their shortcomings. Father God revealed himself to you through these important people, and he continues to do so whenever you remember the good times. A good spiritual exercise when you're feeling low is to ask yourself: "What misconception about Father God is contributing to how I feel?" Then pull up a memory of your dad or mom or someone else (it could be anyone else, including friends) doing something for you or saying something to you that made you feel good. God speaks through such memories. He, too, wants you to feel good.

Father God wants to heal your heart

Jeanie, whom I met through my ministry, told me, "Even though my dad was a good provider, never hit me, and I knew he loved me, I was afraid of him due to how I saw him act in stressful times when things didn't go his way."

No matter how old we are today, for every unhealed wound of the past, there's a little child in us who still cries out to be nurtured and comforted by The-One-Who-Is-The-Perfect-Daddy—the one whom Jesus called "Abba" as he cried out for help during his great emotional agony in the Garden of Gethsemane just before he went to the Cross. We want Abba to hold us in a protective embrace and make every hurt go away.

The problem is, he's invisible. He's not physically touchable. It takes a lot of time and effort to learn how to feel his embrace. In the past, we turned to our human dad and mom (and others) and found them to be insufficient. Humans cannot give us everything we need nor fulfill every longing.

This has handicapped our understanding of the total sufficiency of God. On the one hand, we know that God is quite sufficient for our every need and every good desire. On the other hand, to some degree, each of us sees him as less than he is.

The truth is: God is more sufficient than we can imagine. As Ephesians 3:20 points out, he is able to do *immeasurably* more for us than we could ever ask for or even imagine. And he wants to reveal more of himself to you now.

This book is written to introduce you to Daddy Who Wipes Away Your Tears. In whatever ways your parents and other authority figures have failed to represent Father God's true nature, he wants to enter into your heart more deeply and heal you. He wants to enable you to receive from him more of the goodness and love that you long for. He has been waiting for this day. He is inviting you to reach out to him and accept more from him—more than you know is possible.

Today's Exercise:
List the Hurts You Want God to Heal

To get started, in the left column below, make a list of the ways you've been hurt or failed by parents and other authority figures (teachers, clergy, etc.). Don't dwell on what's painful, just jot them down and then move into the next chapter. As you proceed, your Loving Father's healing embrace will be unveiled.

List every imperfect trait that you've experienced from your human father. You can also do this with regards to your mother, a boss, or any other person in authority over you.

The traits could be long-term personality traits or short-term, temporary traits that were triggered by unusual circumstances. Add it to the list if it got stuck in your memory, because anything that has not been forgotten is very likely affecting your relationship with the Father.

For example, words you might choose are: absent, not a good listener, abusive, short-tempered, too demanding, liar, or undependable.

If you have trouble getting started because you had wonderful parents and were never hurt or disappointed by any authority figure, follow Bill's example:

"I sat in front of my "list" page in order to write down my late father's imperfect traits—not that he was overweight, etc., but significant ones. I looked at that page, and looked, and thought: He was a good Dad, a great Dad. He was strict with us four boys and he smoked, but I couldn't think of anything to write. He developed some new traits as he neared his final 85th year, but I didn't hold him as responsible as I do frailty and senility. But then I thought: I ought to put myself in that left column and re-think the exercise. I did and found several items to list."

So, feel free to think outside the box when writing inside the box of your writing exercise. What are the quick answers that come to mind when you read these questions?

1. Recall a time when you suffered because of someone's behavior. Name that behavior.
2. Think of a time when you felt disappointed, let down, or discouraged. What negative trait(s) caused that problem?

3. What traits in yourself or in others have worked against hope?
4. Did/do you live with anyone who made promises that were insincere?
5. Who made/makes you feel inferior? What trait(s) caused that feeling?
6. Who has been deceitfully charming or manipulative in order to get his own way?
7. Did any authority figure in your life demand respect without earning it?
8. Have your plans or dreams been squashed by a bully or control freak?
9. Were you frequently criticized and belittled?
10. Did you have to "walk on eggshells" when talking to a parent because you were unable to be open and share yourself freely?
11. Was a parent so lost in alcohol or other addictions that you didn't get the attention you needed?
12. Did a parent have unpredictable mood swings, one minute happy and sweet and the next minute throwing a temper tantrum, thus making the gentle side unreliable?
13. Did anyone show cruelty, inflicting physical harm on you or someone else in your family or pets?
14. Which of the following traits were missing from your relationship with your dad? If he was absent from your life, apply these questions to the closest father substitute.

- Was he your hero? A man of courage, perseverance, and integrity?
- Did you feel secure and safe?
- Did he live humbly?
- Did he teach you how to pray and have faith in God?
- Did he teach you the truth about the wrong messages of the world?
- Did he provide you with a moral compass and teach you how to exhibit high moral values with courage?
- Was he the voice of reason when you had problems, offering solutions or a new perspective?

After pondering these questions and any others that come to mind, use the left column (only the left column) to write a list (each five words or less) of everything that describes your father's human imperfections. You may expand this to include any important parental figure. And don't get stalled by your emotions. As difficult and sad as this exercise might feel now, forge ahead. In the next chapter, your healing will begin.

_____

_____

_____

_____

_____

_____

2

Healing Your Image of God's Fatherhood

Jesus made known to us what the Father made known to him. He calls us "friends" because we are the Father's friends. The way Jesus loves us reveals to us what Abba-Father is like. We long to be embraced by and protected by his Fatherhood, but there's a disconnect we need to overcome. So, Jesus wants to give us healing from the wrong images we have of God's Fatherhood.

> *No one knows who the Son is except the Father, and no one knows who the Father is except the Son and those to whom the Son chooses to reveal him. (Luke 10:22 NIV)*

Which Person of the Holy Trinity feels closest to you? Who has the deepest relationship with you? Whom do you turn to first?

For most of us, it's not the Father.

Jesus is our Friend, our Brother, our Savior. He's the center of our worship during Mass. He's the one we receive in the Eucharist. We can easily visualize him by reading the Gospels. We're reminded of what he did for us every time we gaze upon crucifixes in church and at home. Jesus has been the subject of artwork far more often than any other Person of the Trinity—he was so human!

Perhaps it's the Holy Spirit who's the most difficult to feel close to. The Holy Spirit is, after all, *called* a "spirit," and this sounds so ethereal, so other-worldly, so intangible. And yet, if we've been through a Life in the Spirit Seminar or if we've had other experiences of good faith formation about the Third Person of the Trinity, he is the one we rely on for understanding and wisdom, for the right words to speak as Jesus promised (see Luke 12:12), and for help in our efforts to grow in holiness. The Holy Spirit is known as The Helper—how nice!

God the Father is the scary one. We think of him as the one who punishes us when we sin. We believe that he expects perfection from us. And he's too far away up there in Heaven to help us with our little daily problems. Right?

I had a wonderful relationship with Jesus since my earliest childhood, as far back as I can recall. I grew up believing that Jesus was my Best Friend. When I felt lonely, I turned to Jesus. When I felt misunderstood by my father, Jesus sat with me in my room while I cried on my bed. When I forgot a homework deadline and felt panicked and sick to my stomach about it, I knew that Jesus loved me anyway. He encouraged me to do better, building my confidence (not my guilt).

God the Father, on the other hand, could increase my guilt (a mistaken idea that we'll cover more fully in future chapters). I thought of him as The Big Disciplinarian. He loved me, of course, in the same way that all parents who discipline their children are loving them when they scold and dole out punishments. I reasoned that, because I got enough discipline from my dad, why should I spend any time with God the Father? My parents didn't offer me friendship, so it never occurred to me that I could have a friendship with God as my Father. Jesus was the one for that.

I learned early on that Jesus said in John 15:15, *"From now on, I call you my friends. You did not choose Me; I chose you!"* This meant a lot to me because (for example) in gym class I was usually the last kid to be chosen for sports teams. I was sure that the team captains would have preferred to not choose me at all. But Jesus, the God who came to save the world, chose me. ME! Jesus wanted me for a friend. Wow!

However, this was a very limited understanding of John 15:15. I missed the point that Jesus was making about the Father. Read the whole verse: *"I no longer call you servants, because a servant does not know his master's business. Instead, I have called you friends, for everything that I learned **from my Father** I have made known to you"* (NIV, emphasis mine).

The reason why Jesus calls us "friends" is because he *learned this from his Father.* In fact, everything he taught he learned from the Father. Jesus made known to us what the Father had made known to him—because we are the Father's friends.

Let me put this another way. Jesus had a friendship with his Father—not just a sonship. And what Jesus had, Jesus gave. If we are a friend of Jesus, it should be easy to experience friendship with the Father. But this was unimaginable to me.

Like many who are reading this, I never experienced a close friendship with my dad. The idea of confiding in him, and feeling heard and understood like I experienced with my true friends—this was a concept that was so foreign to me, I didn't even imagine it.

So, neither could I imagine that God the Father could be a friend.

The spiritual director I had when I became an adult recognized the importance of this problem. She led me through a visualization in which Jesus introduced me to the True Father. In my prayer-imagination, I "saw" Jesus greet me at the door to the throne room of

God. He opened the door and invited me in. I walked on a red carpet crossing over a vast, shiny floor. Then I arrived at the base of an enormous throne.

Sitting on the throne was a very big Father. I expected a stern expression. But he was smiling at me! Then, with the gentlest of voices, he invited me to sit on his lap. How could I? He was too large. He offered to lift me up, and when I gave him my hand, suddenly he seemed very reachable. The next moment, I was cuddled by him like a beloved child. I could feel the fabric of his kingly garments. I could feel the warmth of his chest against my cheek. I could feel the love in his heart. No question about it: I was loved. I was his beloved little girl.

That experience was the beginning of a Father-daughter friendship that has deepened ever since. It was the first step in the healing of my image of God's Fatherhood. There have been many other milestones along the way. I'll share them with you as we proceed through this book.

Right now the Father wants you to know that you are his beloved child and he is favoring you with an opportunity for true friendship. He says to you, *"You are precious in my eyes, and honored, and I love you. Do not be afraid, for I am with you"* (adapted from Isaiah 43:4-5).

The Father is giving you total love and kindness and mercy. "And so we know and rely on the love God has for us. God is love. Whoever lives in love lives in God, and God in them" (1 John 4:16 NIV). Love isn't love apart from God. Love is God actively giving himself to us. Even the love we have for others is God loving them through us.

Chapter 2: Healing Your Image of God's Fatherhood

It's impossible for God to be untrue to himself. Therefore, he loves us even when we don't deserve it. *"He makes his sun to rise on the bad and the good, and sends rain on the righteous and the unrighteous"* (Matthew 5:45). As Bishop Robert Barron points out: "The sun doesn't ask who deserves its warmth or its light before it shines. It just shines, and both good and bad people receive it. Neither does the rain inquire as to the moral rectitude of those upon whom it showers its life-giving goodness. It just pours—and both just and unjust people receive it."

The Father gave us Jesus so we won't have to face punishment for our sins. *"For God did not send his Son into the world to condemn the world, but to save the world through him"* (John 3:17 NIV).

The Father cares about us so much that he gave us a way to escape from the punishment we deserve. *"This is how God showed his love among us: He sent his one and only Son into the world that we might live through him. This is love: not that we loved God, but that he loved us and sent his Son as an atoning sacrifice for our sins"* (1 John 4:9-10 NIV).

"The Father of Jesus Christ is love, right through. That's all God is; that's all he knows how to do. He is not like us: unstable, changing, moving from one attitude to another. No, God simply is love." (Bishop Robert Barron)

He is completely patient with us regardless of how imperfect we are. Scripture tells us to think often of his kindness, tolerance, and patience, because the kindness of God leads us to repentance (see Romans 2:4). God knows that we overcome sin much more easily through his kindness than through punishments.

He's intimately and infinitely concerned about our daily trials. *"Blessed be the Lord, who daily bears us up; God is our salvation"* (Psalm 68:19 ESV). And *"the Lord knows how to rescue the godly from trials"* (2 Peter 2:9 NIV).

So, why doesn't it feel like he's this wonderful? It's because our image of his Fatherhood has been tainted. We see him through eyes that first saw the imperfections of human parents. We need to differentiate human traits from divine traits. We need to stop projecting onto God that which is not godly. We need to make ourselves available to the truth so we can let God heal our image of him.

God can only be known by our hearts, the center of our soul, where love resides. He cannot be known by the mind because he is much more than we could ever imagine: much better, much more caring, much more available to fill in the gaps left by insufficient human love. To grasp the "more" of him requires that we abandon all of our incorrect ideas, images, and concepts of God. To enter into his healing embrace, we must overcome misconceptions. We must stop projecting human images onto the Abba-Father.

Chapter 2: Healing Your Image of God's Fatherhood

God is not your enemy

"I blame God for being stuck where I am spiritually," Felisha told me. "He gives me as much as I deserve, which in my mind isn't much." Insight into why she thinks this way is found in understanding her childhood: "I struggled to make my parents proud of me, and God is even harder to please than they were! I have loads of experiences from my past that I am sure contributed to this idea that I won't receive much from God. I pray daily, but always as a beggar at God's feet, expecting little help from him—obviously the damage from my childhood is real."

Felisha received her first images of what God the Father is like from parents who were hard to please. They loved her, but—like all parents and every other human being—insufficiently.

She felt loved but *conditionally*. She heard the message, whether it was intended or not, that she should always "do as we say or else…." The "or else" was a discipline that made her feel crushed and stripped of her self-esteem.

"The damage began in my childhood," she continued, "but certain other experiences also helped reinforce the idea that I couldn't be special to anyone. The same is true of God. I must obey or else. Since I am far from perfect and fail him hundreds of times a day, how could he possibly love me very much when I don't love myself very much either?"

This happens all over the world. Gift Nyirenda in Malawi (central Africa) said, "My father was the least person I liked in our family. I thought he was always watching out for new mistakes from me so that he could give out proper punishment. That blinded my image of who God the Father really is, and even after my father's death it is still hard to reconcile my life with the reality [of who God is]."

Every person has injuries and scars from being loved incompletely during childhood—even if our fathers completely earned the "Best Dad" trophies that we gave them for Father's Day and even if our mothers were saints who stayed on the pedestals we hoisted them onto during early childhood.

At the very least, they punished us (we were imperfect, too!) and this didn't feel good. It's nearly impossible for a child to understand that punishment is not a withdrawal of love. We were disciplined for our own good, but at the time it happened, we focused on how good it would feel to continue doing whatever the punishment was trying to stop. The person punishing us was, at that moment, our enemy (because he or she was "against" us). Thus we unwittingly developed an unholy fear of God as Father: The implication is that he's our enemy, not a benefactor, when we sin.

No wonder people stay away from the Sacrament of Confession! And yet, there is no shame in this sacrament. There is healing—reconciliation—with God. There is power. There is a very special gift from God: the supernatural grace to grow stronger in resisting the sins we confess.

"You have been my help ... my father and my mother have forsaken me, / But the LORD will take me up. / Teach me Your way, O LORD, / And lead me..." (Psalm 27:9-11 NASB).

God becomes our enemy only if we become his enemy first—deliberately opposing him, doing whatever we want to do, following our own idea of what is right and wrong—knowing full well that God has a different idea. And since enemies are to be feared, thinking of God as the enemy explains why so many people who prefer the ways of the world are so hard to evangelize. They don't want to have a relationship with God. They fear him and so they get angry at anyone who represents God and his ways.

It's true that God does get angry. We see it in the Old Testament. We see it in the New Testament when Jesus drove the greedy merchants out of the temple. God gets angry when others hurt us without remorse. God gets angry when he watches his children suffering from the terrible repercussions of sin.

However, if we want to be holy, we need to recognize that God is for us, not against us, even when we sin (see Romans 8:31). He appreciates the remorse we feel and our determination to do better. This is the true Father. And so we need to heal our image of God as a father who gets angry at us or pulls away from us whenever we fail to be his perfect child. If the father figures in our lives were unhappy with us because we failed to live up to their expectations, our tainted image of God tells us that he, too, is unhappy with us.

Likewise, if our dads died during our childhood or left the family or traveled often for their jobs, we unconsciously assume that Father God, too, won't be close when we need his help. Lyra grew up without a father. He had died when she was two years old. How do you suppose this affected her relationship with God? As you read her story, look for the imperfect traits of the humans in her life that became a false image of God's Fatherhood:

"My mother became our 2-in-1 parent, providing for all our needs. Because my mother was not home most of the time, she would warn us to be good always or else God would get angry. That was how I have perceived God: a punitive one. I thought we're supposed to earn God's favor. For me then, God was a distant Father who would grant my prayers when I'm good and punish me when I failed."

Imperfect trait #1: Her father was absent. The image of God that this implied: The Father is distant. God is not the doting Father she needs and longs for.

Imperfect trait #2: Her mother could not be home whenever Lyra needed her. The implication: God the Loving Parent is not closely involved in our lives, not available to reassure us when times get tough, and not aware of all our needs.

Imperfect trait #3: Her mother described God as a Father who watches for his children to fail at being good and gets angry as soon as they do. Implication: God only answers our prayers when we earn his approval by being perfectly good, and if our prayers are not answered, then that's proof that we're bad. Since Lyra was imperfect, she could never be good enough for God. She could not rely on his help, which is a false image that was reinforced by imperfect trait #2 above.

Have you ever thought something like this? "God is a good Father, all powerful and all understanding, but what if I am in this mess is because it's me who is at fault? I'm not good enough in his eyes. I miss all his blessings because I am lazy, pleasure-seeking, greedy, envious, selfish, etc. And worst of all, now it's too late and no prayer can change the situation."

Lyra says, "I blamed my father for dying early. I blamed God for letting all the unfortunate things happen to us, and I blamed myself for being inadequate. It took me forty-four years to discover God's unlimited and unconditional love. I had limited him by locking him in a bottle: I treated him like a magic genie who grants my wishes if I've been good."

She continues, "Now that I have finally found a relationship with him, the desire to know him more gets greater every day. Now when I cry to him, it's not because I want to blame but because I need rest and healing. Although sometimes I still fail to trust him fully, when I cry my heart out to him, he makes his presence felt in various ways that I could never have imagined. He truly is a loving Father."

Healing begins

The first step in the healing process is to see yourself the way God sees you: with perfect love. Keep in mind that the Devil does not want you to know the truth. We have an enemy who uses our wounds and traumas and brokenness to do all he can to obscure the Lord's goodness and the Divine Love that's flowing—already flowing!—into your life in a deeper way. Our enemy wants us to doubt God's goodness and love. But God gave us the Divine Word (the Bible) to make the truth clear. For example:

> *Love is patient, love is kind. It does not envy, it does not boast, it is not proud. It does not dishonor others, it is not self-seeking, it is not easily angered, it keeps no record of wrongs. Love does not delight in evil but rejoices with the truth. It always protects, always trusts, always hopes, always perseveres. (1 Corinthians 13:4-7 NIV)*

In other words, God is saying to you right now:

I love you so much that I'm happy to be patient with you! No matter what you've done wrong, I long to give you My kindness. I am not like those who rejected you because they envied you. I do not boastfully lord it over you like others have done, but as your Lord I do boast to the angels and saints about how wonderful you are. Yes, I know how messed up you still are, but when I look at you, I look through the sacrifice that My Son made for you. Your sins were nailed to that Cross, and because you love My Son, that makes all the difference. On My Son is what is ugly about you. I see what is beautiful in you.

I am humble of heart in all of my dealings with you. I will never dishonor you before others—regardless of what you have done. When you fail to see Me as I really am, I am dishonored by it but I am not self-seeking; I am you-seeking. When you sin, instead of becoming quickly angered, I consider how much you want to be holy and I smile about the future because you will conquer this sin with the help of My Holy Spirit. When you ask Me to forgive you, your sin is wiped from the Book of Life; I no longer keep a record of what you did wrong. And before you repented, remember that trouble you got into that felt like a punishment? I did not delight in that. And when you realized the truth, I rejoiced.

No matter what you've done wrong, as long as you humbly turn to Me now and surrender your will to My Divine Will, I am at your side to protect you. I trust you far more than you trust yourself. And no matter what you're still doing wrong without yet repenting, I always have hope in you. My love for you will pursue you all the way, if necessary, to the moment when we meet at the gates of Heaven and we can finally and fully embrace in that perfect love for which you have been deeply longing.

The second step in the healing process is to realize that we are all loved incompletely, insufficiently, imperfectly by the humans who are called by God to love us as much as he loves us. And we love them incompletely, insufficiently, imperfectly, too. To find the joy and peace and healing that comes from God's perfect love, we need to identify the imperfections of humans and turn them into a powerful reminder that Father God is better and bigger than all that. They are, in fact, evidence that he is reaching out to us. He is using them to invite us to realize that only he can give us the fullness of love and goodness and help for which we long. Abba-Father wants us to depend only on God (and here I speak of the fullness of God, the entire Trinity).

We long for the fullness of God's love because we instinctively know that we're supposed to have it. *"I have loved you with an everlasting love"* (Jeremiah 31:3 NIV). He designed us to know and receive his love. He created us because he has been loving us everlastingly, timelessly, desiring to have a precious Father-child relationship with us ever since and *before* we were conceived in our mother's womb. *"For you created my inmost being; you knit me together in my mother's womb"* (Psalm 139:13 NIV).

Our Divine Father brought us into existence so that he could love us with his whole heart, his whole soul, his whole mind, and his whole strength. Jesus told us to *"love God with all your heart, with all your soul, with all your mind, and with all your strength"* (see

Mark 12:30) because this is the nature of God! This is the kind of love he has for us. For *you!*

Father God wants to heal your wounded heart. As he says in Jeremiah 31:3-4 (adapted for this moment): *"I have loved you with an everlasting love; I have drawn you close to Me with unfailing kindness. I will build you up again, my precious child."*

He is with you right now to correct the bad messages that have cut you down. Let him point out your goodness and your giftedness. He sees your goodness even when you cannot. Yes, he sees your sins, too. Yes, he sees your every flaw. But because you have allowed Jesus to be your Savior, when the Father looks at you, he sees you through the filter of the Son's sacrifice on the Cross. He sees your sins nailed to the Cross. He sees you as the cleansed saint that the Sacraments have re-created you to be.

Psalm 139:14 (NIV) is a prayer you might want to say every day if you need healing from a bad self-image: *"I praise you because I am fearfully and wonderfully made; your works are wonderful...."*

Why is it hard to imagine that Father God sees us as so wonderful? Because childhood punishments and the imperfect views of us that came from parents and other father-figures have tainted not only our image of God but also our image of ourselves. True, we sin and make plenty of mistakes, and fail in other ways. But we are much more than that, and God knows this better than we do.

So, if the first step toward healing our image of God's Fatherhood is to embrace the imperfections of others as a reminder to expect perfection only from God, then the second step is to embrace our own imperfections as learning experiences, realizing that God is delighted to help us become who he designed us to be: wonderful masterpieces made in his image.

The third step is to distrust our memories. They are not giving us an accurate picture of God.

Memories are unreliable. They are tainted by our emotions and desires and fears. For example, children usually remember only part of what the parents did or said. And what they do remember is tainted by their partial understanding of their parents' motives. So, it's not surprising that my son remembers trying to get my attention and being pushed away.

The reality is: I worked from home as a freelance writer so that I could be readily available to the children. Ralph and I sacrificed expensive vacations and other big purchases for this. But my son was too young to understand this. In his thinking, if he could see me, he could get attention from me. However, we had rules about interruptions. Whenever I got writing assignments, I had deadlines to keep and I tried to teach my children to respect this.

Thus, when a child needed my attention, if the interruption would disrespect my work, I would say, "No, not right now," and I would give him or her my undivided attention as soon as possible. My son only remembered me saying, "No." His emotional needs were not met fast enough to satisfy his youthful impatience, and so his emotions highlighted the part of the conversation that he disliked the most. As time passed, this emotional highlighting became what psychologists call "implicit" memory.

We all have implicit memories that differ from reality. The problem is, our implicit memories not only affect our relationship with our parents (or whomever triggered the emotional reaction), they also interfere with our relationship with Father God. Accurate or not, what we remember is what we project onto God.

Therefore, **the fourth step** toward healing is to consciously differentiate our human parents from God the Perfect Parent. Ask yourself: What is my image of God the Father? Who is he to me?

In workbook #3 of *The Father's Heart*, we will go a lot deeper into healing. But it starts here. Right now you are laying the groundwork for the healing that you've been praying for.

Today's Exercise:
The Box of Differentiation

Here's an exercise that will introduce you to God the Father as he really is. Look at the list you wrote in the previous chapter, the hurts you want God to heal. In the right column next to each imperfect trait, list the opposite trait. For example, next to "absent" write "always with me." Next to "abusive" you might choose to put "safe." In the example that Bill gave about his dad's old age senility, he wrote, "God is ageless and changeless in all his traits."

Do this now and then continue reading. Trust me, it will be more effective if you don't read ahead.

Pause reading this chapter here.
Return to the previous chapter to complete the exercise.

After filling in the right column, read out loud the list you put there, beginning with "God is…." For example, "God is always with me. God is safe."

What you've just accomplished is the very important therapy of differentiating humans from God and earthly parents from your Divine Father. You've stopped projecting onto God what humans have modeled.

Use this list as a meditation and repeatedly mull over each trait that you named in the column on the right. One at a time, ask yourself: How fully do I believe that God the Father is like this? Mark which ones you need to understand more fully. Then ask Jesus to introduce you to this Perfect Daddy. Visualize it with your imagination during prayer. Invent your own divine throne room or any other scene where it feels good, safe, and friendly to meet the Father. And remember this place! Revisit it whenever you want to feel close to your Divine Daddy.

The final step toward healing is to let God fill in the gaps left by human imperfections. This began for me during a major crisis of faith. I was certain that God had abandoned me and my family.

God, why have You abandoned me?

Ralph and I wanted to move to a better neighborhood so our two young children could grow up in a safe environment. We prayed confidently for our house to sell quickly. Eight months later, our house was still on the market. I wondered: *Why is God ignoring us?* I couldn't shake the sense that he had abandoned us.

Surely God could see what this long wait was doing to our family.

One Sunday on the way to church, I pointed out a house that had sold in just two weeks. I said, "Our house is at least as good. Why do all the other houses sell except ours? We asked for God's help from the very beginning. But did that make any difference?"

Ralph shook his head. "The guys at work never ask for his help and everything seems to work out great for them."

I replied, "I feel like if we had never asked for God's help, we would have sold our house a long time ago." Our faith was eroding fast.

When we arrived at the church parking lot, I stared at the doors. What would I do if I couldn't find God in there? The feeling of being abandoned had been growing over the past several weeks.

We entered the building and were greeted by Sister Cathy, who had been praying for us. She asked, "Have you sold your house yet?"

"No," I answered and hurried on before the tears could flow. Taking a seat, I prayed, *Oh God, let me know You haven't abandoned us. Show me that You're going to answer our prayers.*

Then the Mass began. The congregation sang, "I am your God. No longer be afraid. I know your every need; My love will never end."

My voice cracked and my eyes blurred with tears. My soul cried out, *But I am afraid, Lord! I'm afraid what I want isn't important to You. In all this waiting I feel only torment. Your love never ends for everyone else. God, why have You abandoned me?*

I barely managed to stay in church. To keep from weeping, I thought about a needlepoint project I was designing at home.

Finally, Mass ended. On the way home I told Ralph, "I don't know if I'll be able to go back next week. This feeling that God is ignoring us is destroying my faith, maybe beyond repair. If God doesn't do something soon, I can't see how I'll ever be able to trust him again."

Ralph silently gripped the wheel.

I continued. "Intellectually, I believe God is holding up the sale of our house for some good reason that only he knows. But spiritually, I feel abandoned. If only I could hear God assuring us that it's all for the best."

That afternoon two couples came by to look at the house, but again, no one wanted to buy it. The next day we got a call from the woman who owned the house that we hoped to buy after selling the old one.

"Any interest on your house yet?" she asked.

"No."

"A family came through here yesterday. They really like the place. They'll probably draw up a contract this week. You know I'd rather sell it to you, but I'll have to take the first good offer I get."

"Well," I tried to laugh. "If your house really is the one God thinks is best for us, they won't buy it." I said it more out of habit than belief. Inside, I was panicking. We were going to lose the house we wanted because God was ignoring our prayers.

After I hung up, my heart thumped forlornly while my hand still cradled the receiver. I needed someone to talk to. I needed help overcoming this crisis of faith. But whom could I call? Who had enough faith and was willing to listen to me?

I remembered my brief encounter with Sister Cathy. She had seemed genuinely interested and she had counseling skills. I called her and set up an appointment for Tuesday afternoon.

Another wait. Tuesday afternoon came slowly and I spent the time wondering what my faith would be like when all this waiting was finally over.

As we sat together at the kitchen table in her convent, I told Sister Cathy why I felt so discouraged.

"Depression is anger turned inward," she said. "Who do you really feel angry toward?"

I shrugged. "God, I guess. But I know I shouldn't. It's just that, well, it seems like he answers everyone's prayers but mine."

"Sometimes we project toward God images or feelings we have toward friends. For example, a son who's never known his father's love often finds it hard to understand God's love."

That made sense, but I couldn't see how it applied to me. It wasn't my family or friends who were interfering with the selling of our house. It was God.

Driving home, I thought about what she'd said. I wondered, *Have I ever felt abandoned by friends?* Yes. There were times when I'd been hurt because my friends had let me down.

"But God's not like that!" I exclaimed. "He's a Friend with a capital F, the only true Friend!" The real source of my problem became clear. Because friends had abandoned me, I expected God to do the same. But God is not like human friends!

As if a switch had been thrown, I saw God in a whole new light. Joy flooded in and replaced months of depression. It was still another month before we sold our house, but for the first time, I was able to wait without worry. In the end, we got our proof that God had never abandoned us. We sold our house for a better price. God saved for us the house we wanted. And mortgage rates had dropped.

More than that, the timing was also perfect for the family who bought our old house and for the one who sold us our new home. In the end, my faith was stronger than ever.

3

The Name of Abba, Like No Other Name

There are many names for God in scripture. Let's look at the one that Jesus used: Abba. Then let's find your own special name for God to help heal your relationship with him.

> *For those who are led by the Spirit of God are the children of God. The Spirit you received does not make you slaves, so that you live in fear again; rather, the Spirit you received brought about your adoption to sonship. And by him we cry, "Abba, Father." The Spirit himself testifies with our spirit that we are God's children. (Romans 8:14-16 NIV)*

My dad has a favorite memory about my childhood, which he likes to retell often. It was the day I became old enough to notice the man who was preaching up front in church. I stood up on the pew, pointed and exclaimed, "That's my daddy!"

My dad was the pastor of a Protestant congregation. He beamed with pride at his little girl's pronouncement, even though I had interrupted his sermon.

Unknowingly, I had preached my own sermon that day with those three simple words. As Abba-Father's children, we have good reason to exclaim every single day, "That's my Daddy!" If you're not already doing this, let's begin. It will make a difference.

Imagine that you're sitting in church and the pastor finishes reading the Gospel passage and looks up at the congregation, ready to explain what you just heard. Suddenly the image of an elderly gentleman transposes itself over the pastor. The pastor is hidden completely. What you see is God the Father. You know it's him. No doubt about it! Your innermost spirit recognizes him.

God himself has come to explain the Gospel passage!

His voice is calm, soothing, and gentle yet full of certainty. You can see in his face that he is yearning—deeply yearning—for everyone (even the small children) to understand what he is saying. You have never before heard the Bible explained with such clarity. How beautiful he makes the truth sound! Even the part that used to be difficult for you to believe as true, now you know for sure that it is true and you feel very blessed to finally see it from God's perspective. You can't help but smile and nod your head as the truth sinks in.

Your smile has caught his eye. He looks directly at you and returns your grin with the biggest, happiest smile you have ever seen. You can feel his gaze penetrating deeply into your soul. You know he can see all your faults, but he is still grinning with delight! He sees everything that is good in you and (you know this with all of your heart) he is very pleased with you.

As he turns back to the rest of the congregation to continue the homily, he winks at you.

Now you feel like standing up and shouting, "That's my ___!" Daddy. Father. Papa. Abba. What name do you use? Your choice can affect your confidence in him.

We have emotional attachments to certain names. Who was your favorite person during childhood—someone who cared about you, someone you enjoyed, someone who was safe and uplifting?

When you meet a new acquaintance with the same name today, do you automatically have good feelings about this person?

Who bullied you?

A stranger today with the same name might have to wait for you to process your inner distrust as you carefully watch for proof of goodness. Though this process might happen so quickly you don't realize you're doing it, it's a normal psychological phenomenon.

At around the age of six, I stopped calling my father "Daddy" because it seemed to express a warmth between us that existed only in my wishful thinking. Nor did I want to call him "Father" because that sounded too formal, too cold and stand-offish, and my relationship with him was better than that.

What does the name "Father" feel like to you? What does praying to "Our *Father* who art in Heaven" do for your desire to feel closer to God? Does this name exude trust? The kind of trust that dwells in your heart and affects your behaviors?

Trust does not reside in your intellectual-thinking head where you know the truth about God. How much of your life—your daily decisions, moods, and words—gives evidence that you trust God? Trusting him so much that you would follow him across a dangerous highway while traffic is speeding toward you?

A prayer life based on intimacy with the Father

Many people don't know that God is speaking to them every day in a fatherly way. Do you recognize when he's hugging you and comforting you and is being everything else that we look for in a daddy?

Charmaine calls him "Papa God." She says, "Some years ago I remember coming home very distressed from my job, crying out to him, and he scooped me into his bosom to comfort me. If only I could have stayed there! Recently, I asked him for a hug. I received it in the arms of a complete stranger. The next day, the Holy Spirit confirmed that this had been the hug that I had asked for."

That's my Daddy! And yours, too.

When I need a hug from God, I sometimes return to the throne room where I had first climbed onto his lap. Visualizations like this are very helpful, especially after prayerfully asking the Holy Spirit to anoint your imagination. I also visit my Divine Daddy in the visualization of a sunny, green field surrounded by colorful wildflowers. In this meditation, the Father is sitting on a quilted blanket on the ground. He's inviting me to join him, and I do. He already knows what's bothering me, so I snuggle into his embrace and let him hold me.

This is more than just a mental exercise. It's very real. I'm sure of it, because I always feel better afterward.

When you imagine being alone with Father God, where do you go? What does the scene look like? The more details you add to what you visualize, the more effective the meditation becomes.

When you finish the encounter, do you feel more loved? Do you feel heard? Do you feel like you benefited from the experience? If so, trust those feelings. If you had been unable to force yourself to feel better before meeting up with the Father, you can be sure that the reason you feel better afterward is because you really, truly did spend time with your divine Daddy.

But what if you cannot imagine being alone with Father God? What if your attempts to meditate on and feel his presence keep failing? Remember that Jesus said (John 14:7 NIV), *"If you really know me, you will know my Father as well. From now on, you do know him and have seen him."* So, focus on Jesus and let him reveal the Father to you. Listen to Liddy's story and see the Father in Jesus:

"I recall when I was very young, probably in my teens, that I felt so unloved (in my family of 6, I was the 5th child). I was crying uncontrollably on my bed and I wished God would take me Home. I didn't belong here on Earth. Then something made me turn and look behind me. There was the figure of Jesus with outstretched arms! And this wonderful peace filled me. He did not touch me or hold me, and when I looked again there was nothing. But this peaceful love enfolded me."

God as Liddy's Father reached out to her through her relationship with Jesus.

One of the clues that God is speaking to you in a fatherly way is what happens when you feel heard. As you pour out your grief to God—your tears or your troubles—how do you know that he is truly listening?

To answer this, consider: Was your human father a good listener? And your mother and the priest in the confessional and others you've turned to when you needed to be heard? Could you approach each of them with confidence in their desire to believe you and understand you and listen to your heart as well as to your words?

If you can say yes to that last question, you probably have no difficulty feeling heard by God. You're very blessed! Many who are reading this have not had the same experience. Yet.

God, of course, hears every word we say and every thought we don't speak. He understands us better than we understand ourselves. And he sees it all through the lens of "the big picture"—the entire situation, including the needs of everyone who's affected by it. He knows what's transitory and he knows how to lead us into the eternal if only we would respond to his voice.

A very important part of being heard well is receiving well the responses that come to us. We learn to do this—poorly or appropriately—from our human relationships. If the father-figures in your life have genuinely listened to you and understood you, it's likely that you find it fairly easy to entrust your heart to God and believe that he cares. And you behave accordingly.

The best possible scenario is when the person we're speaking to is strongly connected to the Holy Spirit, actively listening to both the Spirit and to us at the same time. When that happens, we can trust that God will speak to us through that person.

But ask yourself this: Do you have any automatic *distrust?* A built-in protection mechanism that keeps you guarded in case the other person does not really have your best interests at heart? If you do, it's affecting your ability to receive all that the Father wants to give to you and say to you through this other person.

Consider what it means to be truly heard. A lot of people seem to be listening to us, but if they become judgmental about what they hear, they have not listened well. When we feel misjudged after being open and honest, it's because the person we're talking to is listening more to his or her own ideas, faults, and presumptions than to us.

How has this affected your relationship with God?

Felisha, who says she never feels "the comfort of his closeness," described her father as a good listener but very judgmental and her mother as extremely controlling and more judgmental toward her than to anyone else. When asked what her stumbling block is in her relationship with God, she answered with frustration, saying: "I can't understand how a loving Father, seeing a child of his trying to reach him, would not bend down and pick her up."

There's a direct connection between how her parents "listened" to her and why she thinks that God ignores her when she reaches out to him. She did not learn what being listened to is really like. She says, "I know that God listens when I speak to him, but he is like one of those people we see on TV who waves away journalists, saying 'NO COMMENT!'"

Judgmentalism creates a very wrong impression about God. God is, of course, the ultimate Judge. Psalm 75:7 (NIV) says, *"It is God who judges: He brings one down, he exalts another."* Saint Peter preached that everyone has to *"give account to him who is ready to judge the living and the dead"* (1 Peter 4:5 NIV). However, if we think of ourselves as deserving of punishment even after we repent, we've forgotten why Jesus died on the Cross.

This train of thought is actually from the Devil. Satan is the Accuser, not God. Satan wants us to feel so bad about ourselves that we believe God can't or won't be gentle with us. Satan does not want us to realize that God is, in truth, a loving Father who bends down into our sinful messes to pick us up and cradle us gently next to his heart.

Yes, Abba-Father is The Judge. But that does *not* mean he is judgmental.

Judgmentalism teaches that God doesn't care about us nearly as much as he cares about laws and rules and regulations. Judgmentalism teaches that God does not hear our hearts, that he does not consider our motives, and that he does not notice how much we actually desire to be holy even though we are sinning.

In reality, a good judge listens very well. A good judge takes everything into consideration. Psalm 119:137 says, *"You are just, O Lord, and your judgment is right."* God is never judgmental but he does make fair judgments—more accurate judgments than any human can make. His heart goes out to everyone who genuinely wants to be lifted from sin. When he sees his child reaching up to him to be pulled out of her messes, of course he bends down to pick her up!

For our relationship with Abba-Father to be healed, we need to unlearn what judgmentalism taught us and learn how to recognize God the Father as the Good Judge. Then we will be able to proclaim with delight: "That's my Daddy!"

Find your special prayer-name for God

We know that God is supposed to be completely trustable, but when your prayers are not answered, how do you feel about God (not *think*, but *feel* about him)? Do you feel abandoned? Ignored? Rejected? To whatever extent we feel this way about God, that's how much we don't trust him. And how do you suppose that makes *him* feel?

Chapter 3: The Name of Abba, Like No Other Name

Servant of God Luisa Piccarreta (1865-1947), also known as the "Little Daughter of the Divine Will," was an incredible mystic. Jesus told her:

> I feel sad when they think that I am severe, and that I make more use of Justice than of Mercy. They act with Me as if I were to strike them at each circumstance. Oh! how dishonored I feel by these ones. … by just taking a look at my life, they can but notice that I did only one act of Justice—when, in order to defend the house of my Father, I took the ropes and snapped them to the right and to the left, to drive out the profaners. Everything else, then, was all Mercy: Mercy my conception, my birth, my words, my works, my steps, the Blood I shed, my pains –everything in Me was merciful love. Yet, they fear Me, while they should fear themselves more than Me. (June 9, 1922)

Remember, Jesus revealed God the Father through the way he treated people. Like Father, like Son. Re-read what Jesus told Luisa Piccarreta, but this time recognize the feelings of Abba-Father.

Now think of a prayer request you've recently offered up to God. Imagine making the same request to the person who was your best childhood friend. Let's further imagine that this person has been given supernatural powers. Knowing how good and caring your friend was to you, what do you suppose he or she would do with your request? And probably pretty fast, too, right?

Okay, so try nicknaming God with that person's name. My best, longest childhood friend was Mary Cleary. It just doesn't seem suitable to pray to God and call him Mary. It does help, however, to project onto God the qualities about Mary Cleary that I enjoyed so much.

It was my friend Mary who introduced me to the fun of bowling. "You'll like it," she told me.

"Let's go!" I trusted her. I believed her. No question about it, I would enjoy bowling. So, I asked my dad for permission and he told me, "No."

Oops, my dad had disappointed me again. I felt personally rejected when he rejected my request. Making matters worse, he offered no explanation.

As a teenager, I had become bold when Dad's responses made no sense to me. So, I demanded to know, "Why not?"

Of course, he didn't like this and responded with anger. I began to cry. Finally, the truth came out: He said he was trying to protect me. He didn't like bowling because he wasn't good at it, and he was sure that I wouldn't like it either.

Joe had a similar experience:

I'll never forget when my father and mother forbade me from joining the Boy Scouts. My heart was set on it, but what my father didn't understand, he didn't permit. I blamed him for being an ignorant immigrant who never got to eighth grade. It wasn't until much later that I realized the big picture: His love was protection from what he didn't know and understand.

God as our Good Father wants to protect us, too, but unlike our human parents, God understands everything. When he says no to us, he's taking into consideration the big picture—the *whole* picture. How it would affect our future. How it would affect others. Whether or not it will lead to sin.

We need to remind ourselves of this whenever we allow old wounds, consciously or unconsciously, to project onto God the limited knowledge of humans.

Happily, my dad changed his mind when he heard himself explain his reason for saying no to my desire to go bowling. And guess what! I enjoyed bowling very much despite all the gutter balls I rolled. If I had trusted my dad's feelings about bowling, though, I would have felt discouraged by my low score. But because I trusted my friend's enthusiasm for the game, I enjoyed it immensely. That's what a best friend can do.

It's taken me a lifetime to see Abba-Father as a best friend. Some grown-up daughters have a best-friend relationship with their dads. I can't imagine what that's like. If you have the same difficulty, it's time to be healed from relating to Father God as if he were a disciplinarian who has limited understanding and limited compassion. It's time to develop a relationship with him that's a close friendship. A good friend doesn't reject you over bad bowling. And this is the kind of friendship that the Divine Father wants to have with you.

It's very healing to project onto God the loving traits of the best friends we've known. Did your friends understand you when you shared your deepest thoughts with them? Abba-Father understands you better than all others. Did your friends ever criticize you when you were open and vulnerable with them? Your Divine Father does *not* do *this*, but if there is something to criticize, he wraps you in his loving arms and invites you to improve without making you feel bad about yourself.

Did your childhood friends enjoy hanging out with you? What about the friends you have today? Why do they feel good in your presence? Abba-Father likes being with you for the same reasons.

Which friends have been strong supports for you? Like: "I've got your back. No matter what others think of you, I'm on your side." Abba-Father is definitely saying that to you right now.

How do I know this is true? Because I rely on it! For example, whenever someone falsely accuses me or refuses to believe me, my first reaction is to defend myself. I want to argue in an attempt to change the other person's mind. (A normal human reaction, right?) But I've learned that this rarely works. More importantly, I need to stop caring about what others think of me and focus only on what God thinks of me. Instead of trying to protect my reputation (which is what motivated me to argue), I should let Father God protect me.

When I turn to him and ask him to defend me, everything changes. God's love fills me and this brings with it a peace that is inexplicable. Sometimes the other person hears or receives the truth from God that I had wanted to argue them into believing. But when they don't, it doesn't matter because God is comforting me. I visit him on the blanket in the field and tell him what the other person accused me of. I do this with insecurity, because I wonder if there is any truth to the accusation. "Maybe I feel defensive because I don't want to hear the truth," I tell him. "What do You think about me?"

And then, if there's a wrong I need to admit and fix, Abba-Father reassures me that I am much more than this one sin or this one mistake. He reminds me of what is good about me, what the other person had failed to see in me. His perfect love fills the entire conversation.

I'm able to do this healing meditation because I've had good friends who defended me.

Making the connection between our friends' loving traits and God's is an excellent spiritual exercise. However, we can't take this so far as to use their names when praying to God. That would sound silly and be too distracting. And yet, names are important. Think about how you feel when you contact an important person (a boss, the leader of your favorite ministry, the owner of a business you've sent a complaint to, and such), and you get a reply that includes your name—not in some formal way (like "Dear so-and-so"), but embedded in the message itself. It indicates that you matter. You feel connected.

God says to you, *"Do not fear, for I have redeemed you; I have summoned you **by name**; you are mine"* (Isaiah 43:1 NIV; emphasis mine). When you summon God by name, what do you call him? Does it make you feel connected? And connected closely enough?

Remember what I shared with you, in Chapter 1, about why I could no longer call my father "Daddy." The name didn't fit because it felt too intimate, so I chose "Dad." I considered calling him "Father," but that was too formal. This carries into my relationship with the Divine Father. I can't call God "Dad" because that totally projects my human dad onto him. The name "Father" seems too formal. And the name "Daddy" is tainted by memories of feeling disappointed in and disconnected from my dad. So, what name would help me in my relationship with God the Father?

What works for me might not work well for you. For some people, the name "Father" conveys loving respect while for others it makes God seem distant. A good step deeper into the Father's heart is choosing a name for him that summons all the wonderful and perfect fatherhood that you long for.

What did Jesus call him during those private all-nighters of deep prayer? It seems likely that he called him "Abba."

"Abba" was the Aramaic word for "father" in the traditional liturgies and prayers of the Jews whenever they referred to God *in a family context*. It did not literally mean "Daddy"; it had no connotation as a term of endearment or a child-like relationship with God. It was simply what sons and daughters called their dads throughout their lives.

The Gospel writer Mark tells us that Jesus used this name for the Father while agonizing in the Garden of Gethsemane. In great emotional angst, Jesus called out: "Abba! Father! All things are possible for You; remove this cup from Me." And then he added, *"Yet not what I will, but what You will"* (Mark 14:36 NASB). Since "abba" means "father," it's as if Jesus cried out, *"Father! Father!"* Interestingly, it's only Mark who shows Jesus using the name Abba; what was Mark's reason for pointing this out? What did he intend to teach?

One of the reasons why Jesus was killed is because he closely aligned himself to God the Father. He repeatedly emphasized that he came from the Father and did and said only what the Father wanted him to do and say. His opponents thought, "Blasphemy! Jesus is merely human like everybody else. It's impossible that he could be both human and divine at the same time."

In using "Abba! Father!" as the cry of Jesus, Mark wrote both the Aramaic word for "father" and the Greek word. His use of the Aramaic name "Abba" referenced the Jewish liturgies that Jesus had grown up with. By coupling this with the everyday Greek word for father, Mark was reaching out to both Jews and Gentiles, making it clear that God was the same God for both. And Mark was saying that God was not only the father of Jesus, he was *The* Father—the Father of us all.

This very pointedly asserts that God's Fatherhood was very important to Jesus, both theologically and in the family sense—including in the hour of his greatest emotional need. Look at the depth of trust this implies: "Abba! Father! All things are possible for You; remove this cup from Me; yet not what I will, but what You will."

When you pray the Lord's Prayer, "Our Father, who art in Heaven...," do you feel that same level of deep trust? I don't—not automatically. But when I pray, "Abba, my True Father, my Divine Daddy in Heaven...," what a difference this makes!

Maybe you'd prefer to call him Papa or Pops or Paw. Choose a name that is powerfully intimate for you, a name that does not remind you of your own human father unless he doted on you so much that he really was a good representation of the compassionate trustworthiness of God.

There are two more times in the New Testament when God is called "Abba." Paul used it in Galatians 4:6 and Romans 8:15 to emphasize the special son/daughter relationship we have with the Divine Father who loves us so much that he adopted us into his family. It's an adoption that gives us full privileges and inheritance. (We'll get into this more deeply in a later chapter.)

In other words, God is trustworthy in a very fatherly way and in the best sense of the word "fatherly." The *Catechism of the Catholic Church* helps us understand this (in paragraph 239):

> By calling God "Father," the language of faith indicates ... that he is goodness and loving care for all his children.... The language of faith thus draws on the human experience of parents, who are in a way the first representatives of God for man. But this experience also tells us that human parents are fallible and can disfigure the face of fatherhood and motherhood.... He transcends human fatherhood and motherhood, although he is their origin and standard: no one is father as God is Father.

Meditating with Our Father

We can learn much about who God the Abba-Father really is by meditating on the words Jesus gave us when he taught us how to pray:

Our Father,

> Abba, Papa, my perfect Daddy, the same Father who sent angels to minister to Jesus in the Garden of Gethsemane...

Who art in Heaven,

> because You are divine, You are Creator of all, You fathered me, gave life to me and want to spend eternity with me, because

Heaven wouldn't be the same without me, and You long to enjoy it with me…

Hallowed be Thy name,

for Your very name is holy and You want me to call you "Abba-Father," sanctifying the title of Father, teaching me and showing the world what true fatherhood is meant to be…

Thy Kingdom come,

because You have adopted me and honored me with the privilege of being Your prince/princess, generously giving to me the inheritance of all the valuables of Your Kingdom, and You desire that I live in this inheritance right now…

Thy will be done,

because everything You will is good and everything You desire for me is blessed…
On Earth as it is in Heaven,

because You care about every nuance of my earthly life, every moment, every problem I face, every person I meet, every opportunity to use the gifts and talents You have given me…

Give us this day our daily bread,

because You care about every hunger I have and You want to feed me with the nourishment that satisfies, purifies, heals, and blesses me. You want to give me Your Son, Jesus, Who is the Bread of Life, Who is teaching me to trust You more by making me rely only on You, one day at a time, moment by moment...

Forgive us our sins as we forgive those who sin against us,

because it pains You to see me enslaved to my sins and chained to the sins of others, since You want only what is good for me...

Lead us not into temptation but deliver us from evil,

for this is what I truly want, and You as my Abba-Father want to protect me and strengthen me in the midst of the evils of this world. You want to rescue me through Jesus from demonic strongholds and influences...

Amen!

Saint Francis of Assisi meditated on the nature of Abba by writing his own prayer inspired by the Our Father prayer:

O OUR most holy FATHER
Our Creator, Redeemer, Consoler, and Savior,

WHO ARE IN HEAVEN:
In the angels and in the saints,

Enlightening them to love, because You, Lord, are light
Inflaming them to love, because You, Lord are love
Dwelling in them and filling them with happiness
because You, Lord, are the Supreme Good,
the Eternal Good
from Whom comes all good
without Whom there is no good.

HALLOWED BE YOUR NAME:
May our knowledge of You become ever clearer
That we may know the breadth of Your blessings
the length of Your promises
the height of Your majesty
the depth of Your judgments.

YOUR KINGDOM COME:
So that You may rule in us through Your grace
and enable us to come to Your kingdom
where there is an unclouded vision of You
a perfect love of You
a blessed companionship with You
an eternal enjoyment of You.

YOUR WILL BE DONE ON EARTH AS IT IS IN HEAVEN:
That we may love You with our whole heart by always thinking of
You
with our whole soul by always desiring You
with our whole mind by directing all our

intentions to You and by seeking Your
glory in everything
and with our whole strength by spending all our
energies and affections
of soul and body
in the service of Your love
and of nothing else
and may we love our neighbors as ourselves
by drawing them all with our whole strength to Your love
by rejoicing in the good fortunes of others as well as our own
and by sympathizing with the misfortunes of others
and by giving offense to no one.

GIVE US THIS DAY:
in memory and understanding and reverence
of the love which our Lord Jesus Christ had for us
and of those things that He said and did and suffered for us.

OUR DAILY BREAD:
Your own Beloved Son, our Lord Jesus Christ,
AND FORGIVE US OUR TRESPASSES:
Through Your ineffable mercy
through the power of the Passion of Your Beloved Son
together with the merits and intercession of the Blessed Virgin
Mary
and all Your chosen ones

AS WE FORGIVE THOSE WHO TRESPASS AGAINST US:
And whatever we do not forgive perfectly,
do you, Lord, enable us to forgive to the full
so that we may truly love our enemies
and fervently intercede for them before You
returning no one evil for evil
and striving to help everyone in You.

AND LEAD US NOT INTO TEMPTATION:
Hidden or obvious,
Sudden or persistent.

BUT DELIVER US FROM EVIL:
Past, present, and to come.

Amen.

Today's Exercise:
That's my Daddy!

Now write your own version of the Our Father prayer, and finish off each sentence with the exclamation, "That's my Daddy!" For example:

Our Father, You are in Heaven where You see everything that is going on in my life, and because You care so much about me, You are working a plan for my benefit, not disaster.

That's my Daddy!

Hallowed be Thy name. I worship You because You are holy.

That's my Daddy!

And so forth.

By writing it down, it becomes much more meaningful. Meditate on it daily. Bring it to mind when you're reciting the Our Father prayer in church where we go through it too fast for a deep meditation. Once your own version becomes so well known to you that it floods your worship when the recitation of the Our Father begins, you'll automatically become cognizant of Abba's nearness. And your heart will exclaim, "That's my Daddy!"

_____
_____
_____
_____

4

Words That Make a Difference

What words do you use that imply something about God that really came from the ungodly traits of the humans in your life? This is what we'll look at now because it can make all the difference between a safe, healthy friendship with Abba-Father and a relationship that's handicapped by misconceptions.

> *"Because of the devastation of the afflicted, because of the groaning of the needy, / Now I will arise," says the LORD; "I will set him in the safety for which he longs." / The words of the LORD are pure words; / As silver tried in a furnace on the earth, refined seven times. (Psalm 12:5-6 NASB)*

The Christmas of my first bicycle was both delightful and frustrating. Delightful because I finally received what I'd been begging for. Frustrating because my younger sister got a bike too.

Whenever I had pleaded, "*Please* can I have a bicycle," my parents told me that I wasn't old enough. So, you can imagine how I felt when my sister got her bike the same day I did, even though she was two years younger than me.

"Unfair!" I cried.

I can empathize with the first laborers in Jesus' parable about the vineyard workers (see Matthew 20:1-16). The landowner hired them early in the morning and agreed to pay them a denarius (the usual wage for a day's work). He hired more workers at noon, still more at mid-afternoon, and a few more just one hour before quitting time. Then the landowner, a.k.a. God, paid everyone the same amount. In relating this to my bicycle, I had "worked" longer than my sister at growing old enough for a bike.

"Unfair!" cried the men who had worked the longest. "Some of those other guys worked only one hour and paid them the same amount you gave to us. That's not fair!"

But the employer replied, "I am not being unfair to you, friend." (Friend? Is this how God treats his friends? As Saint Teresa of Jesus said, "If this is how You treat Your friends, no wonder You have so few of them.")

Jesus continued the parable, still sounding very unfair, with the landowner saying: "I gave you what you agreed to. So what if I want to give those who were hired last the same as I gave you? I can do whatever I want with my money."

Very unfair! Hmm, that even sounds like my human father scolding me for being unhappy about waiting an extra two years for my bike. It also sounds like God is being tricky. Even miserly. As if he's saving money by cheating his full-time workers out of what they deserve.

And then comes the stinger: "Or are you envious because I am generous?"

Yup, that's me! I commit the sin of envy every time God makes easy for someone what I have worked hard for or prayed many years for. The little girl who waited too long for a bike has become the lady who cries "Unfair!" at the blessings of others.

You see, while I'm waiting on the Lord to give me what the Bible assures me he has promised, I'm vulnerable to the idea that God doesn't care about me as much as he cares about others. I can usually resist this false message, but not when I see someone else get what I want.

But what does the word "fair" really mean? To my parents, it meant treating everyone equally. My dad often reiterated that it was very important to him that he treats each of his three children equally. This meant, on that particular Christmas morning, that both me and my sister got our first bikes at the same time. I knew that this was not the true definition of "equal." To be treated equally, my sister and I would have been given our first bikes based on age, not "at the same time."

Thus, my image of God became: He is a Father who is unfair while claiming to be fair.

So, let's ask: Does "fair" mean the same thing to Father God as it did to my human father? And to you and me?

What point was Jesus making with this parable? To find the answer, we have to look past the way the parable makes us feel when we put ourselves into the work shoes of the first laborers. Jesus is revealing the Father's compassion toward the underdog. The disadvantaged ones.

Consider the type of person who often gets turned down when applying for a job: the weak, the sick, the disabled, the "too" old and the "too" young, and other targets of discrimination, such as criminals or anyone with a bad reputation. Jesus is asking you: "In what ways do you feel discriminated against? The Father is going to give you more than what anyone else would give you! Who has overlooked you? The Father is going to give you special treatment! Who has rejected you because you don't match their expectations or because they don't understand your capabilities? The Father has a special mission for you."

Turn off the auto-responses that control your feelings

If our focus remains on the first laborers of the parable, we miss the opportunity to learn that God wants to give us more than what's "fair." That's the trouble. We get stuck in feelings that are based on wrong images of God's Fatherhood.

Malformed unconscious beliefs control us with auto-responses that are inappropriate for the situations that trigger them. We need to take control away from the misconceptions that have been limiting our understanding of Abba-Father.

The image of God as a Father who is unfair is, in fact, very unfair to him. This is *not* who he really is. He is a caring Father who is genuinely interested in you. He is generously doting on your unique needs. He is concerned about you while also remaining concerned about everyone else in your life. He gives you what you are ready to receive as soon as you are ready for it. He is never late, not even when we think he is. His timing is always perfectly suited for our lives and for the journeys of our faith growth.

However, it's possible to know this as a fact and yet not as a belief. Here's an example of how this happens:

God has taught me the truth of his perfect timing for many years. It's uncanny how often he reveals his hand in the timing of nearly everything I do. Despite this, sometimes I react to circumstances instead of act on what I know is true. My auto-response tells me that the Father is a God who answers prayers with, "Okay, you can have what you want, but first you'll have to wait until someone else catches up." It tells me: "Anyone else who might be impacted by your prayer request has to reach the point of asking for it, too, wanting it as much as you do. Until then, you have to wait." In other words, I think that I'm handicapped by the spiritual handicaps of others.

"Unfair!" I cry.

We have a lot of misconceptions about how our Divine Father treats us. These mistaken ideas often come from words that have been tainted by misuse, such as "fair." Another tainted word is "love."

Nancy didn't know the real meaning of love. Despite several years of therapy for the abuses she had suffered during childhood, she needed spiritual healing to discover God's love for her. She needed to learn that God's love was different than what she had grown up with.

Her father had been mentally unstable. When Nancy was five years old, he was committed to a psychiatric hospital. After that, one of her older brothers began to molest her and another brother physically and emotionally abused her. The image of God she unconsciously learned from her dad was that he is a Father who is not there to defend you when you need him most; he is not protective. From her brothers, she learned that love means being a victim. When she heard the words in church that describe Jesus as Victim, she identified with him but in a painful, non-healing way.

Furthermore, her mom often said while spanking the kids (just like many other parents do because it's true), "It's because I love you that I have to do this to you!" So of course, to Nancy, all love was suspicious. Even God's.

She says, "To this day, I have trust issues." When her second husband molested her daughter, "That was the final straw. I felt, right then and there, that I couldn't trust *any* male. I wanted to die, and I made my final attempt on the highway." Thanks to the therapy she received, her suicidal impulses were overcome, but she needed to learn how to trust God. She could not do that without first learning that there are men who are trustworthy.

After she came to me for spiritual healing, I introduced her to my husband, Ralph, and we included her in some of our family activities. We wanted to show her what God's love is really like. I led her through some inner healing exercises, and these began to make a difference. However, she distrusted my love for her. She wondered, "When is the abuse going to start?" To protect herself, she tried to push me away with anger and false accusations.

Of course, the abuse she expected from me never happened. But that didn't stop her from reacting to me as if I were about to hurt her. Our friendship was a minefield, and it didn't take much for an explosion to get triggered. Despite learning that I was safe, her emotional auto-responses over-ruled her intellect. And the same auto-responses also affected her understanding of how God loves her.

Meanwhile, the Holy Spirit inspired me to stand my ground patiently, quietly, calmly, and Jesus gave me the strength to do it. When time and again I did not treat her in the harmful way that she expected, she began to understand the difference between the manipulative, so-called "love" of her childhood traumas and the safe, unconditional love of Abba-Father.

Words of love do not mean the same to the abused as they do to the non-abused. More than anyone else, those reading this book who've been abused (especially during childhood) have more to overcome, more to reprogram, more to learn and relearn about who Abba-Father really is and what his love is truly like.

Nancy and I talked a lot about the true meaning of love and how God designed relationships to be. We differentiated Abba's unconditional love from every other relationship she'd ever had. Over the course of several years, she learned the truth about love, forgot it when circumstances triggered auto-responses, relearned the truth, and gradually became stronger in it.

It took a lot of reprogramming to deactivate the bombs in her minefield, and today there are still situations that trigger unhelpful auto-responses. She's had to repeatedly practice what she learned. She's had to persist in reexamining her auto-responses, relearning the truth, and reinforcing appropriate responses. It's a learning curve that needs to continue for the rest of her earthly life. She explains:

> Trust is an imprint that we learn as young children. We trust Mom and then Dad. When those building blocks are missing, trust has to be a conscious effort, done every day. It never becomes natural after those imprinting years are long over. Unless God comes in and does a miracle, trusting others has to be put on just like someone who, after losing his legs in a car accident, has to put on prosthetic legs in order to walk. It's a lifetime struggle. I will never trust the way a child in a safe home learns to trust. I have accepted this fact

and I do my best to just trust God because he is the most important figure in my life. As for trusting others, I lean on my crutch of trusting him first. But it will always be a struggle for me, just like a person who has to live a life with no legs.

If she hadn't persisted through spiritual healing with determination and the help of a professional therapist, she never would have made the progress that she did. And then, to continue progressing, Nancy relied on constant prayer, the Bible, spiritual books and talks, and Holy Mass: the essential sources of growth for all of us.

Anyone who has been abused needs the threefold approach that helped Nancy: (1) psychological counseling from a qualified therapist, (2) persistence and determination and conscious effort, and (3) spiritual healing. Without these, it's common to get stuck in the auto-responses that control our feelings.

Rout out your misconceptions about Abba-Father

All of us—everyone—can deepen our relationship with Father God and increase our trust in him by paying attention to our auto-responses whenever it seems like God is not loving us the way he should. Even the words that we rotely and obediently recite in church can trigger wrong ideas. For example, when the intercessory prayers of Mass and other group events are read, how does the congregation respond? A very common formula is: "Lord, hear our prayer." What happens with that on the subconscious level of faith?

Chapter 4: Words That Make a Difference

The implication could easily be: "Lord, You don't hear us unless we ask You to hear our prayer." Think about it. If this is what you believe, change the formula. Mentally or out loud change it to: "Lord, thank You for hearing our prayers." Do you notice the change in your spirit?

What other words do you use frequently that imply something about God that is simply not true? These nuances can make all the difference between a safe, healthy friendship with Abba-Father and a relationship that's handicapped by misconceptions.

The Holy Spirit has provided us with tools that free us from malformed auto-responses. It's like having a treasure map and a magnifying glass to search for what has been hidden. Only when they are exposed can we conquer them. Let's uncover the subtle, hidden misconceptions that have been influencing you.

God is good. We know that. We profess it out loud. But whether we actually believe it or not is proven in the tests of everyday life. Our reactions to stressful situations—our behaviors during difficulties—reveal a lot about our unconscious beliefs.

For example, do you *really* believe that God is good all the time? That it's impossible for him to sin against you (or against the loved ones for whom you've been praying)? If you do, then why do you get stressed out by the situations that you've entrusted to him?

Or how about this: Do you *really* believe that God is omniscient (all-knowing)? If you do, then why tell him how to fix your problems or how to change your spouse or how to convert your adult child who has left the Church?

Admittedly, we understand Abba-Father imperfectly. So, we compensate by adding to the end of our prayers, "But You know what's best. Thy will be done." Later, our joyless response to the hardships of life betray our inner handicaps. We still have unconscious messages undermining our faith. "Thy will be done" means, deep down, something like: "Thy will be done because I have no say in the matter anyway. Thy will is not fair, but You are God and I cannot control You, so I'm unhappy. Now I'll pray a Novena of the Rosary to get the Blessed Mother to change Your mind."

We accept his will and we don't accept it—both at the same time!

In scripture, God is described as the Rock whose works are perfect. All of his ways are just. He is faithful and he does no wrong. He is upright and just (see Deuteronomy 32:40). In human logic, where one plus two equals three, "God's ways are just" is added to the injustices we suffer even after we pray and therefore equals a definition of "fair" that is not fair to us at all.

Yet we know that God is faithful and does no wrong. We know he is a Father who is always "fair" and "just." So, how do we make sense of the times he seems unfair? We blame ourselves. Our auto-response belief is that we don't get what we want because of God's justice. We don't deserve to be treated better.

This is why our auto-responses can tell us that we must wait for others to become ready for divine help when we give our prayer requests to the Father. They further tell us that we must wait patiently or else we're sinning and the Father gets upset with us.

But who can be patient under those circumstances? It's not our fault that we're ready while others are not. We now have someone else to blame. Hooray.

Every malformed, below-surface thought process hampers our relationship with Abba-Father. Unless we pay attention to what's

Chapter 4: Words That Make a Difference

happening underneath and rout out what is wrong, we remain stuck there. The good news is: Once exposed to the light of the scriptures and the revelations that are readily supplied by the Holy Spirit, they lose their hold on us. Our faith grows.

To enjoy a close, fun, helpful intimacy with the Father, we need to understand him as he really is. We need to reprogram our thought processes and consciously choose to live in the truth of God's goodness. We need to do this repeatedly until we form a healthy, holy auto-response.

Reprogramming involves understanding the scriptures better and reading them in the context of the bigger picture or lesson that's connected to them. This is what we've been doing with the parable of the vineyard workers. As I said before, Jesus was revealing the Father's compassion toward the underdog. In this light, "fair" and "just" describe a God of compassion, mercy, and love. I like that! It's not about the bike at all. Nor wages. It's about unconditional, merciful love.

Let's look at how knowing this can affect our prayer requests. When we pray, we can experience the peace that overcomes stress by reminding ourselves that God is fair and just and that therefore he doesn't withhold anything good from us, not even if we've had a long, dark past of doing evil. What matters, in his eyes, is how much—right now—*we* want what *he* wants.

So, what does he want? He wants to say yes to the desires of our heart. He wants to say yes to our prayer requests, as long as what we want is not sinful. But he wants to give us even more than we've asked for. His "yes" might come with a "but not now" or "not this way."

And he wants us to learn something valuable, something that will increase our holiness, something that will also help others. When we want this too, we appreciate how fair Abba-Father truly is. We relax. We discover joy even before our prayers are answered.

The divine logic is: "God's ways are just." Add to this his forgiveness for the injustices that we've repented from, and now one plus two equals "he only wants what's best for me," which equals far more than we can ever imagine. Therefore, "I can trust him with 'Thy will be done' and truly be at peace with that."

The formula is simple: To free ourselves to enjoy a close, trusting relationship with Abba-Father, we must first identify and then clear up our misconceptions about him.

Today's Exercise:
Reprogram your thought processes

To find the errors that control your auto-responses, listen to how you complain. Every complaint carries within it a clue about how you see Abba as less than he really is, such as less caring, less powerful, less attentive, or whatever the "less" is that has been diminishing your relationship with him. These clues are important!

Today's exercise will help you detect the misconceptions that have been affecting you. Write a letter to the Father. Name your toughest prayer request—that situation that has been going on for far too long—and complain to him about how he is or is not handling it. Complain, complain, complain! (This is not sinful; he can handle it and he knows that your innermost desire is to be healed.) Write down why you're upset with him, but if you don't feel upset with him, dig deeper by finishing this sentence: "I trust You, Father, but I wish You would ____."

Write it fast, unfiltered. Be honest. Be brutally honest. Don't hold anything back.

Describe your feelings—they contain wonderful clues. How do you feel about waiting so long for your prayer to be answered? Even if you think you know why God wants you to wait so long, how do you feel about that?

Maybe you're waiting for God to zap someone into loving you the way they should. You know that God won't force them against their free will. So, how does *that* make you feel? God is surely powerful enough and creative enough to get around their free will somehow. But nothing has changed. Or maybe it got worse. Complain to God about his (apparent) lack of intervention.

Write this letter to God now before finishing this chapter. Write it, don't just think it. The second half of this exercise will shed light on what you wrote.

_____
_____
_____
_____
_____
_____
_____
_____
_____

Watch your words

My first spiritual director, Irene Huber, frequently taught that "what you say is what you get." She wanted everyone to pay attention to the words we use, because our choice of words can impact us emotionally and spiritually. In her healing ministry, she had discovered that when people came to her saying, "I'm sick," they were less likely to receive a miracle than if they said, "I've been diagnosed with or have the symptoms of a sickness."

We can either own the illness or take ownership of God's concern and compassion for us in our illness. By choosing our words carefully as we describe what we're seeking from him, our focus shifts from the limitations of the illness to the potential of the healing.

To say, "I have ___," is to admit ownership of it. Which is truer for you? "I have faith" or "I have fear"? Do you have a fear that if your prayers are not answered, disaster will strike? Do you have a fear of God disappointing you? Or any other fear that's based on a misconception about God?

I'm sure you want to say, "I have faith," but when you react to situations that challenge your trust in God, reacting so spontaneously that you don't have time to choose your words carefully, what comes out of your mouth? For example: "I'm feeling very worried about this situation. I'm afraid it's going to get worse." This does not mean you have no faith. It simply means that you're routing out a misconception that's been controlling you.

Look again at the letter to God that you wrote in today's exercise.

1. What did you take ownership of with the words you wrote? (For example: "I have fear that this terrible situation will last forever.")

2. Which sentences can be rewritten to start with "I am ___" or "I have ___"? (For example, change "You know what is best, Father, but I sometimes feel angry about the injustice of it. I can't imagine why You haven't done anything about it yet" to "I am angry because You seem unconcerned about the injustice. I have doubts that You truly care.")

3. What clues about your understanding of Father God do these sentences reveal? (For example, if you wrote "I am angry because You seem unconcerned about the injustice, I have doubts that You truly care," ask yourself: "Which humans in my life treated me unjustly long ago?" And then remind yourself: "Ahhh, but Father God is much better than them! Of course he cares! He hates the injustice far more than I do."

4. Which sentences proclaim correct understandings and which ones are raising flags about misconceptions? (Highlight in yellow what is true about Abba-Father, and cross out the misconceptions. Circle the parts that need further clarification.)

Chapter 4: Words That Make a Difference

Our choice of words when praying to the Father can reveal a lot. In your prayer exercise:

1. Were you demanding or trusting? (Perhaps both?)

2. Did you tell God how to solve a problem? How humble were you in sharing your ideas with him? How much of the problem-solving did you leave up to him?

3. What do your demands (or strong preferences) and problem-solving ideas indicate about your conceptions of God?

4. Which words obscure what Abba-Father is really like?

By unearthing the indicators of a lesser faith, your faith will grow. Identify the wrong messages that some of your words imply. Then seek out the truth from scriptures, a spiritual director, or a friend who has mature faith. Post the truth on sticky notes by your desk and on the bathroom mirror. Turn them into memorized mantras that you repeat often and out loud. This will reprogram your auto-responses.

Rewrite your prayer request with carefully chosen words of faith, even quoting scripture. Let this become your mantra in the particular situation that's covered by this prayer. And guess what will happen! Your new way of praying will improve your prayer words and build your faith during other situations as well.

5

The Safest Father in the World

The path to Heaven is the journey of becoming a little child who sleeps without fear in the Father's arms. How safe do you feel with God the Father? Are you able to climb up onto his lap and into his arms to feel his protective concern for you? He wants you to feel his powerful arms wrapping around you and creating a zone of extreme peace with you at the center.

> *The proof of our existence is that God—somebody who is higher, somebody who is greater—is holding us, protecting us. (Saint Teresa of Calcutta)*

No one is loved fully in any human relationship. This is a normal flaw of the human condition. And it's the source of much of our anguish. It's why Jesus told us to forgive seventy times seven times (see Matthew 18:22); in other words: more than we think is enough. And sometimes we have to do this repeatedly—even daily—with the same person!

Therefore, because we project onto God what we've learned from humans, it's difficult (though not impossible) to fully believe that God loves us completely in every possible way despite our own flaws. It's *especially* difficult if we hold within us any misconceptions about how *safe* God is.

If we fear him at all (speaking not in the biblical sense of the word "fear," which by definition is a very humbling awe of God)—if we fear God for any reason, at any moment, this is a red flag alerting us to our need to discover more about how safe God really is. If we're afraid of being disappointed by his handling of our prayer requests or if we're afraid we're not good enough to receive his doting, fatherly love, we need to open ourselves to what it means to be "safe in God."

For Nancy, whose dad had abandoned the family through mental illness, leaving her unprotected from the abuse of her brothers, feeling safe with God seemed impossible. However, her traumatic childhood was not the only reason why she felt unsafe with the Father. It's the same with us: There are multiple reasons that were layered on top of each other throughout our lives. Healing requires identifying them and turning each of them over to Jesus, one at a time.

Nancy says, "One of the big reasons why I struggled to believe that Father God loved me was because I had asked him to heal my six-year-old niece Shelley, my Mom, and even my ex-husband Buck. I yearned for them to be healed and live. But all three times, God said, 'No,' at best, but worse, I thought he didn't even care enough to hear my cries. They all died! I was devastated."

But then one day as she turned this over to Jesus, he impressed upon her: "Nancy, the goal of life isn't about living a long life on this side of Heaven. The goal is to get on the inside of Heaven's gate. Your loved ones were each asked, and they all gave me their yes to coming Home. They all knew you wanted them to live, and they did live and are alive here and now. Remember, the Kingdom of Heaven is here and now. They are still with you."

Chapter 5: The Safest Father in the World

Nancy explains how this healed her: "Since I believe in life after death, the sting of their death was healed by this realization. Of course, it didn't happen in a day. But over time it did help the healing process."

Let's look at how safe you feel with Father God. Are you able to imagine yourself sitting on his lap? When you pray, are you able to imagine being warmly embraced by him? If not, then the goal of this chapter is to make it possible. Otherwise, the goal of this chapter is to identify any remnants of fear, because perfect love casts out all fear, and God wants you to know that he loves you that much.

There is no fear in love. But perfect love drives out fear, because fear has to do with punishment. The one who fears is not made perfect in love. (1 John 4:18 NIV)

This scripture explains that God, because his love is perfect, drives out fear. He drives it out! He does not use the fear of punishment to convince us to change from sin to saintliness. Let that sink in. This is not what we instinctively believe because every good parent punishes their children when they misbehave.

It's true that we do deserve to be punished for our sins, but Jesus took our punishment for us when he allowed himself to be crucified for our salvation. If we accept his sacrifice as a gift, then we need to realize what Jesus hopes we'll do with the gift. He wants us to live in the freedom that his sufferings obtained for us: freedom to be fully loved, freedom from the fear of punishment, and freedom to enjoy Abba as the wonderful Father that he truly is.

If instead we don't feel safe with God, it's because we have not yet been made perfect in love. Notice that I did not say, "… because we have not yet *become* perfect in love." We cannot achieve this for ourselves. God is the one who perfects us. How? By filling us to overflowing with his perfect love. (Scripturally speaking, the word "perfect" means "complete, full, whole.")

So, if fear controls us in any unhealthy, unholy way, it's a big red warning flag alerting us to the fact that we have not yet allowed God to fill us with his perfect love. He is completely, fully, wholeheartedly in love with us, and we must choose to open ourselves fully to it. That's why you're reading this book. (God is very pleased!) Every time we go to the Sacrament of Confession, we open ourselves more fully to God's perfect love. And it happens in countless other ways too.

By the way, loving others is a lot easier when we first know that we are deeply and totally loved by God.

Abba-Father desires that we go straight to him for the love we seek. No human parent, spouse, or friend will ever love us completely, not until they have entered into the fullness of God's love in Heaven. So, our Perfect Father wants to fill in the gaps. In the Old Testament, he said, *"I have loved you with an everlasting love; I have drawn you with unfailing kindness. I will build you up again…"* (Jeremiah 31:3b-4a NIV).

But wait. I detect a contradiction. Jesus said that whatever we ask for in *his* name, the Father will give it to us (see John 16:23). That means we must go through Jesus to reach the Father, right? Is this because the Father is too fearsome for the direct approach?

For some of us, it might mean exactly that. We feel safer when Jesus is our Mediator. The root of this feeling probably comes from learning that a good mediator can protect us from someone's anger or punishment or disapproval or injustice. My dad was a good mediator when he fielded that late-night phone call from Ralph's impatient father. I'm sure you can think of several mediators during your life who made you feel protected.

Gifford remembers his mother as a mediator. He says, "I used to look at my father as someone to fear, a person I could not request something from unless I reached him through my mother." This indirect approach caused delays that led young Gifford to feel disappointed and depressed. Later, he learned that, during the delays, his parents had discussed his needs. And so he learned that good comes from waiting patiently, because their discussions were based on their love for him.

In other words, by asking his mother to mediate for him, he learned that his father loved him very much. This is what happens when Jesus serves as our Mediator. It brings us closer to the Father. We discover how very much Abba-Father cares about us.

A very healing meditation is to visualize Jesus mediating for you. Start by recalling an incident from your childhood in which you felt unloved. Close your eyes and return to the scene. How old are you? Where are you? How do you feel? What happened that made you feel this way?

Then invite Jesus to come into the scene. What does he say to you? For example, a common punishment is to send children to their rooms. When my parents scolded me for a wrong-doing and banished me to my room, I felt rejected, ignored, and abandoned. I understood where I had erred, but at that moment the only thing on my mind was a deep yearning for at least one of my parents to come to my room and hug me, reassure me that they still loved me, and discuss calmly how I needed to change. And, most of all, I wanted them to affirm what I did right. In other words, I needed Abba-Father's perfect love.

Years later when I brought this into a healing meditation with Jesus, he listened closely to my needs. (By the way, before beginning any healing meditation, pray and ask the Holy Spirit to anoint your imagination. That's key. I'll guide you through this in today's exercise at the end of this chapter. And if what you visualize or hear makes you feel uncomfortable, or if you just can't "see" Jesus because you're not a visual person or for any other reason, quit trying and meet with a spiritual director, or a mature Christian who has an inner healing ministry, or a Christ-centered therapist.)

After I told Jesus what I had needed from my parents when they sent me to my room, I visualized him leaving my bedroom (after asking my permission—God is such a respectful gentleman!) to fetch my parents. He brought them in, one by one, and asked me to tell them what I needed. In this imaginary encounter, my parents listened and then asked for my forgiveness. I gave it to them, we hugged, and I asked God to forgive them too. Afterward, the little girl in me no longer felt like crying about being sent to my room. Jesus had truly healed me through the meditation. And most importantly, I no longer feared that Father God might "send me to my room," a.k.a., punish me by rejecting me and abandoning me.

Today, I don't need to bring Jesus into the meditation. When someone disturbs me or a situation frightens me, I close my eyes and visualize Abba-Father sitting on that blanket in the field of flowers that I described earlier. I run to him, plop myself next to him, and snuggle into his side while he wraps his protective arms around me, smiling at me all the while. I tell him what's bothering me, and I don't leave until he has comforted me with wisdom, reassurance, or simply his wonderful embrace.

Sadly, traumatic experiences make the healing process much harder. If your relationship with the Father has been damaged by trauma, until you work through the healing process, you will probably always feel unsafe with him and you will need Jesus to continue being your Mediator. If you get stuck there, ironically Jesus is separating you from the Father. You have unintentionally placed him *between* you and the Father. The good news is: Since Jesus and the Father are one God, there really is no such separation.

To feel closer to the Father's heart of parental love for you, it's very healing to see Jesus as not only a Mediator but as your *pathway* to the Father.

Jesus wants to help you go straight to the Father's parental heart so you will know how very dear you are to him. Jesus knows that this will fill in the gaps of your human parents' imperfect, insufficient love. He wants you to be able to climb up onto Abba's lap and feel the safety and security of his concern for you. He wants you to feel his powerful arms wrapping around you and creating a zone of extreme peace with you at the center.

Make straight the path to Abba's Heart

John the Baptizer preached, *"Make straight the way of the Lord"* (see John 1:23). To anyone living in Israel at the time, this was a message of safety. Today, we tend to see it only as a call to take no detours on our journey of faith.

In John's time, as it was for Isaiah whom he quoted (*"make straight in the desert a highway for our God"* from Isaiah 40:3), the roads or highways were paths that had been forged by previous generations. They were *not* straight because travelers had to wend their way around hills and dunes. However, danger lurked behind every mound because they might be hiding a thief or an enemy ready to pounce. So, travelers made wide sweeps through potentially dangerous areas, always keeping in view the far side of the hills, allowing themselves room for evasive action.

They took the safest route. Not the shortest route. Heading straight through the area could have been disastrous. So, when Isaiah and John declared that people should make a straight way to the Lord, they were declaring that the Lord was safe.

As mentioned previously, those who were abused during childhood have more to overcome and relearn about who Abba-Father really is and what his love is truly like. The visualization that worked so well for me, when Jesus introduced me to the Father and the Father pulled me up onto his lap, usually does not work for those who experienced trauma, especially when it was physical abuse.

The woman whose brothers began to abuse her when her father was taken from the home (Nancy) had been so traumatized that she could not even go to the Sacrament of Confession. It required being alone with a man, and this triggered severe panic attacks. After many inner healing sessions coupled with weekly counseling by a professional therapist, and by getting to know my husband Ralph as a friend in social outings, she gradually felt safer and safer around men. She returned to Confession and even began to enjoy this sacrament.

Abuse is but one way that a person might be violated. Any behavior from others that disrespects our personal dignity is a violation of who we are as children of God. We're violated when a thief steals from us. And when anyone wrongly condemns us by false accusations, we are violated just as much as the truth itself is violated.

Many years ago, in the front yard of my New Jersey home was a row of evergreen trees that I cultivated. They had reached the height of about seven feet when a car careened around the corner and drove directly into them, knocking two of them down. The driver backed off of them and quickly drove away. The trees survived and are now quite tall and beautiful, but I felt surprisingly very violated.

The car was red, and for days I watched for a red car to pass by my house so that I could track down the driver. I don't know what I would have done had I found him, but it became an obsession. I took walks nearly every day in the hope of finding this car parked in a neighbor's driveway. Although the physical exercise was good for me, the mental exercise was not.

I asked Jesus to help me find this car. He answered the prayer by asking me to forgive the driver. He sternly but gently told me to let go of my need to find him. That was not easy for me. I had to force myself to obey him, but when I did, I received a healing. I no longer felt violated.

Why did tree damage disturb me so much? The damage was not permanent. I only needed to prop the trees up with supports to give them time to recover. What made me feel violated was the unwillingness of the driver to stop and apologize. I wanted him to show me that he cared.

When it seems like God doesn't care about you, what feels violated?

In a subconscious way, the tree incident connected to times when my personal dignity felt violated because someone didn't care about me. It reopened an old wound from the time my dad forgot to pick me up at the shopping mall. I was a young teenager alone, waiting, feeling abandoned and a little scared. My mother didn't drive; I had to depend on my father who was very preoccupied with his work. We had no cell phones in those days, and I did not want to go off in search of a pay phone in case my father showed up while I was away from the predetermined pickup location.

He finally remembered me after he came home from work at the end of the afternoon and realized that I was not there. Undoubtedly he felt bad about forgetting me, but by then I was feeling too frightened, hurt, and mad to realize it. My importance as his daughter had been violated. It felt like he didn't care. Of course, he really did care but being forgotten is a form of personal violation.

When we feel violated, we feel very unsafe. Although my dad never again forgot about me after promising to pick me up, I continued to feel unsafe. Eventually, I matured enough to forgive him so that I could heal. I can now wait for a ride without the fear of abandonment if the driver is late. I've even had other tree incidents (damage of one sort or another done to my property) without wanting to track down the perpetrator to make them apologize. But in my relationship with Father God, I needed to do more than forgive my father before I could feel totally safe.

Keep in mind that forgiving is not only for the benefit of others. It's a gift that you give to yourself. It's the gift of freedom: You will no longer be chained to the source of the hurt. The more difficult giving forgiveness is, the bigger the gift will be because your newfound freedom will be that much more meaningful. But don't try it by yourself. The Holy Spirit will empower you to forgive if you ask for help.

Also keep in mind that forgiving does not mean forgetting. Remember enough to stay safe without dwelling on what happened. By forgiving you will become free to remember without anger, fear, and stress. Then you will be able to find a new pathway to a new place of peace and joy. You will be able to persist in reaching this new place despite what happened to you.

Learning to feel safe with Abba-Father

Have you noticed that it's easier to feel closer to God outdoors in the beauty of nature? It happens this way because creation is an expression of the beauty of God himself. God is more beautiful than we can imagine. Any image of him that makes him seem ugly in any way (such as a grumpy, frowning old man) is a lie from Satan who wants to take over as your father.

To conquer Satan's tricks, find an image of fatherhood that makes you feel safe, and project that onto Father God.

When Nancy was struggling to feel safe with Father God, I asked her if she knew any kind-hearted old men. She thought about this for a while. Unable to identify anyone from her life who fit this description and made her feel safe, she considered her favorite TV shows. She remembered "The Waltons" and Grandpa Walton (played by actor Will Geer). "To this day," she says, "Father God looks like Will Geer to me."

Feeling unsafe with Abba comes in many forms, often without an obvious connection to safety. For example, when we feel frustrated about a lack of opportunities to make our dreams come true, deep down we might be feeling unsafe with God. In my own experiences, it seemed like God gave me talents, training, desires, goals, and dreams and then refused to give me opportunities to use them! At best, he let me use them only partially and only in small ways. I felt like a caged bird prevented from flying with the wings that God had given me.

Here's how feeling unsafe leads to feeling caged: When we've been violated, someone else has taken control—to our detriment. We are imprisoned by the demands they make on us when they force us to do something against our will. They have stolen our freedom to be who we really are and do what we prefer to do.

Forgiving the perpetrators puts us back in control. Regardless of whether or not they are actually remorseful, forgiving them frees us from the control they've had over our thoughts and emotions. And it frees us to heal the damage they've done to our relationship with Abba-Father.

However, to enter into the healing process, we must first identify the wrong perceptions about God that were generated by the lack of safety.

What makes you feel unsafe with God? Has he seemed uncaring? Has he asked you to do something that led to trouble and misery? Did you put into his hands a job interview or house sale or a travel opportunity and then suffer dashed hopes? Did you entrust a loved one to him but he/she died or abandoned the relationship anyway?

Let's look at the proof that God *is* safe and is *always* safe.

1. **Abba-Father never violates our freedom; he never tries to control us.** Proof of this is the free will that he's given us. He never interferes with our freedom to choose sin instead of holiness, even though he wants more than anything for us to be holy like him. Whatever we do, he lets us do it because he has no desire to control us.

2. **Abba-Father has no desire to invade us nor force himself upon us.** Consider the lost souls who remain far from God. He could easily break them in order to humble them, but he waits for them to realize how broken they have made themselves.

3. **Abba-Father never violates our personhood.** Consider how Jesus treated the woman caught in adultery (see John 8:1-11). He protected her from being stoned, which was what the law prescribed for her sin. And then he gently, tenderly asked her, "Where are your accusers now?" After pointing out that

none of them had condemned her, he said, "Neither do I. You are free to go; stop sinning." He acknowledged that she had sinned without disrespecting her dignity.

4. **Abba-Father makes no demands against our will.** Consider the last time the Lord asked you to do something and you opted not to do it. He might have asked through the priest who requested larger donations, or through a call for more catechists that awakened a desire in your heart until you reasoned that you had no time for it, or through an aging parent who needs more help from you. God did not punish you when you said "no." Problems were caused by your "no," but it was not God who caused them. And when you changed your mind and did what he asked, it was not because he forced it. It was because you went through some sort of process that shed new light or convicted you with a genuine desire to say yes. Right?

God does put pressure on us to do things his way. He did issue those ten commandments. Jesus did give a whole sermon about rules (see Matthew 5, 6 and 7). But every rule and every commandment are for our own good. We benefit from behaving the way God tells us to live. Never does he coerce us, though. We are safe with him. Completely safe.

The caged feeling that I suffered was not caused by God. I needed to deprogram my misconceptions about God. So, I focused on the truth: Abba-Father never inspires in me desires, goals, and dreams in order to torture me by frustrating me with closed doors. Other forces are at work: the free will decisions and prejudices of people who failed to believe in my dreams.

Some of the blockages were indeed God's "fault"—a happy fault, a blessing, because the timing was not right yet. I had to learn to see Abba-Father not as a father violating my right to use my talents and training but as a father who cares so much that he protected me from situations that I was not ready to handle. He also protected me from being exposed to what *others* were not ready to handle, for if I had freely proceeded, they would have caused problems that I could not have foreseen.

My cage door finally swung wide open one day during daily Mass. Actually, it felt more like the cage bars dissolved away. This book is one of the results. And although there are still people in my life who are not yet cooperating with God's plans for me, I am safely resting in Abba's lap while we wait together for their progress. It's an active waiting that has kept me joyfully on an adventure of using my talents and training in other ways.

Today's Exercise:
Create a visualization

When you do today's spiritual exercise, start with the idea that, to the Father, you are the only person in the world. Put aside the reality that there are billions of other people seeking his attention. God does not have the limitations that parents have when too many people and tasks and responsibilities prevent them from giving undivided attention to their children.

Nancy says, "I used to pray to God thinking that *if* my prayers made it to the office in Heaven, my message was laying in an in-basket on an angel's desk. Or, if God did get it, that it was in a stack under more important prayers like praying for a war to end or praying for a loved one who was dying. I just didn't think my prayers were his top priority. But when someone told me that, to God, I am the only person he's focused on, then my prayers became more fervent because now I knew he indeed heard them and has put them on the *top* of his list of priorities."

Early in this book I shared the story of how I met the True Father by visualizing Jesus taking me to the Father in his throne room. I also shared with you the imaginary field where I often go to sit with the Father on a blanket in a peaceful field. These are sacred spaces where I am alone with Abba-Father and he is giving me his undivided attention. Do you have a sacred space in your imagination yet? Let's go there now. We'll design one if you don't have it yet.

(1) Pray the following or something like it:

> In the name of Jesus Christ, I offer my imagination to You, Holy Spirit. Anoint my imagination to receive inspired ideas. Help me to visualize a place where I can safely sit with God the Father and feel his love and realize how very precious I am to him.
>
> *Jesus said: "No one knows the Son except the Father, and no one knows the Father except the Son and those to whom the Son chooses to reveal him. Come to me, all you who are weary and burdened, and I will give you rest. Take my yoke upon you and*

> *learn from me, for I am gentle and humble in heart, and you will find rest for your souls." (Matthew 11:27-29 NIV)*

Lord Jesus, reveal the Father to me. Amen.

(2) After reading this paragraph, close your eyes and think about a beautiful place where you feel peaceful. You can use my imagery of the throne room or come up with your own scene. Notice that Jesus is standing next to you. He is smiling at you. He is happy that he can now introduce the Father to you in a new and more truth-filled way. What is he saying to you?

_____
_____
_____
_____
_____
_____
_____
_____
_____
_____
_____
_____
_____
_____

(3) Imagine that Jesus is pointing out the Father to you. What do you see? If you have trouble seeing the Father or if the visualization becomes disturbing, say the name of Jesus over and over again until you feel peaceful. If the peacefulness never comes, stop and set up an appointment with a spiritual director or a Christian therapist who can lead you through this.

_____
_____
_____
_____
_____
_____
_____
_____
_____
_____
_____
_____
_____
_____
_____
_____
_____

(4) Go to the Father. Take your time. Take as much time as you need to approach him and hug him or climb up onto his lap or sit next to him. What do you see? Details are important because they help make the experience more real. (And it *is* real because you asked the Holy Spirit to anoint your imagination.) How bright is the scene? What else do you see? What is the Father wearing? Does he have a beard? Are his eyes sparkling? Is he smiling? Keep adding details to the scene.

_____
_____
_____
_____
_____
_____
_____
_____
_____
_____
_____
_____
_____
_____
_____
_____

(5) Talk to Abba-Father about the fears you still have. Do this within the visualization. Afterward, write down everything you remember saying.

_____
_____
_____

(6) Here's what Abba-Father says in response to you (adapted from Hosea 11:3,8,9).

> It was I who taught you, **[insert your name]**, to walk,
> taking you by the arms;
> though you did not realize
> it was I who healed you.
> How can I give you up, **[insert your name]**?
> How can I hand you over to those who mistreat you?
> My heart is overwhelmed;
> My compassion is stirred up.
> I will not give vent to My anger,
> nor will I destroy **[insert your name]**;
> For I am God and not a man,
> the Holy One who is with you.

And he is saying to you:

Be Satisfied with Me
(attributed to St. Anthony of Padua)

Everyone longs to give themselves completely to someone,
To have a deep soul relationship with another,
To be loved thoroughly and exclusively.
But God, to a Christian, says,

"No, not until you are satisfied, fulfilled and content
With being loved by Me alone,
With giving yourself totally and unreservedly to Me,
With having an intensely personal and unique relationship
With Me alone.
Discovering that only in Me is your satisfaction to be found,
Will you be capable of the perfect human relationship
That I have planned for you.
You will never be united with another until you are united
With Me alone,
Exclusive of anyone or anything else,
Exclusive of any other desires or longings.

I want you to stop planning,
Stop wishing,
And allow Me to give you the most thrilling plan existing,
One that you cannot imagine.
Please allow Me to bring it to you.
You just keep watching Me, expecting the greatest things.
Keep experiencing the satisfaction that I Am.

Keep listening and learning the things I tell you.
You just wait.
That's all.
Don't be anxious.
Don't worry.
Don't look at the things you think you want;
You just keep looking off and away up to Me,
Or you'll miss what I want to show you.
And then when you are ready,
I'll surprise you with a love far more wonderful than any
You could dream of.
You see, until you are ready and until
The one I have for you is ready
(I am working even at this moment to have you both ready at the same time),
Until you are both satisfied exclusively with Me
And the life I prepared for you,
You won't be able to experience the love that
Exemplified your relationship with Me.
And this is the perfect love.

And dear one, I want you to have this most wonderful love,
I want you to see in the flesh a picture of your
Relationship with Me,
And to enjoy materially and concretely
The everlasting union of beauty, perfection and love
That I offer you with Myself.
Know that I love utterly.

I Am God.
Believe it and be satisfied."

6

The Father Heals Us of Fear

In today's world, more and more people fear God due to the lifestyles they have chosen and the decisions they have made. Their inner child thinks they will be punished, and shame tells them that they need to hide from God. At the same time, Abba is reaching out with the love of a father who knows that erring children need extra attention, while Jesus the Savior is actively and continually seeking the lost sheep who are hiding from the Father.

What are you ashamed of? Does thinking about it make you want to run to the Father or away from the Father?

> *Then the man and his wife heard the sound of the Lord God as he was walking in the garden in the cool of the day, and they hid from the Lord God among the trees of the garden.* (Genesis 3:8 NIV)

Fear is our enemy. Not God. Abba's love is the cure for all of our traumas and every fear, every worry, every anxiety. The safe and perfect love that we do not receive from humans is readily available from him. Do we really believe this? It seems that most people do not.

It's not something that is taught often enough in religious education classrooms, homilies, and adult faith formation events. I've met many good, faith-filled people who are ridden with anxiety. The reason, in many cases, is that we tend to expect—even demand—

that our peace and joy come from other people doing what they are called to do (i.e., love as they should with the love of Christ).

A wife expects her husband to love her faithfully, listen to her because he cares, and humbly apologize when he's wronged her. The husband expects his wife to be supportive of him in his trials, love him no matter what mood he's in, and humbly apologize when she's wronged him. The truth is: This is the love that God calls for in the Vocation of Marriage, so of course it's expected. The fact is: Everyone fails. Humans will always disappoint us.

Only God's love is perfect. And it requires spiritual and emotional discipline to turn to him and let his more-than-enough love become our more-than-enough peace and joy.

Abba's touch is very healing, but people run and hide from it. And yet, despite their best efforts to make a good life for themselves, hiding from God actually increases their fear, worry, and anxiety. If they don't recognize this as a wake-up call but continue trying to hide from the God who sees all and knows all, their thought processes become irrational. Their inner soul, which knew God from the day of their conception, is in conflict with their minds and their wills.

As Saint Augustine so famously said to God, "You arouse us so that praising You may bring us joy, because You have made us and drawn us to Yourself, and our heart is restless until it rests in You."

Felisha, who in chapter two said that her parents were hard to please "and God is even harder to please than they were," was ruled by fear, anxiety, and negativity from a very young age. "I was a sad and very pessimistic person," she says, "even though I didn't really have a reason to feel so bad all the time, especially not in later years."

Then, as an adult, she heard a talk on the subject and continued to seek and listen to several more. It changed her life. "I thank God that I no longer wake up every morning with dark clouds obstructing the light in my life," she says.

One of the tools she learned to use is scripture: She finds a verse that speaks to her fears and repeats it aloud to herself until the fear loses its hold on her. Later in this chapter we'll cover other ways we can let Abba-Father heal us from fear.

The downward spiral of fear

By God's grace and love, we learn to overcome all of our fears. However, to receive his grace and live in the joy of his love, we need to stop fearing God. This is hard to do if we've been crippled by shame.

It happens even in the best of families. A child is raised in a church-going family with Christ-centered values. As she enters into adulthood, she chooses to accept the ways of the world that are contrary to the ways of God. So, she begins to hide—she hides from the truth and she hides from God and she sometimes even hides from her family. What she's really trying to do is hide from is the contradiction of choosing a lifestyle that was not part of her upbringing.

For many, this leads to becoming inactive in the faith. Deep down, they know that something is wrong in their relationship with God, but shame tells them to be afraid of him. They feel safer not going to church. They feel more and more uneasy around churchgoers. They might even become argumentative in order to justify their faithless decisions. If you know someone who's like this, remember that the louder they argue, the more fearful they are of the truth that they're hiding from.

Fighting for their right to be wrong is a form of hiding that we see a lot of today. Consider what might happen to those who adamantly fight for abortion, gay marriage, gender change, and other controversial moral issues. What if they choose to open their minds to the possibility of being wrong? What if they were to investigate what the Church teaches about these issues? What if they even went so far as to humbly examine why the teachings are really for their benefit, how they are based on love, and how they make the world a better place when implemented?

Unless they also know that Abba loves them unconditionally, many feel terrible shame about the wrong beliefs they have been clinging to. Unless someone helps them realize that seeking forgiveness would free them to enter fully into his love, most fight shame by becoming more adamantly opposed to whichever truths make them feel uncomfortable. And unless they reach out for God's mercy and learn how to receive it, most are afraid (often pushing this fear down into their subconscious) of crumbling under the weight of their own self-disapproval. They are fighting off poor self-esteem or depression, and what they don't realize is that they are really fighting against the Father who highly esteems them.

In other words, their fear of God sends them into hiding from the very Father who can provide everything they need. But facing the truth—with fear standing in the way—can be a very difficult struggle. Meanwhile, the world is telling us to not struggle with it but to give in to the desires of our flesh-nature. In fearing shame, they don't know the secret to becoming shameless.

In Matthew 15:21-28, a Canaanite woman with a demonized daughter goes to Jesus for help. The disciples try to shoo her away. Even Jesus apparently dismisses her. But she is "shameless" about persisting with her request, and Jesus approves. Saint John Chrysostom extolled her as a model to emulate: "[She is] shameless with a goodly shamelessness." Unlike this single-minded mother, he pointed out, "When we fail to obtain, we desist; whereas it ought to make us more urgent."

The Canaanite mother exemplifies the proper attitude toward God: a combination of humility and boldness, of deference and defiance. This is a combination that leans on God's goodness and depends on close intimacy with him.

It's not easy to reach this point when we're hiding from God, fearful of the truth. For example, the parents of aborted children who are willing to face the truth about what they have done need to find their way to God's mercy, but it's such a terrible truth that it's easy to fall back into self-protectively arguing that abortion is a good choice.

Similarly, the young man or teenage girl who feels attracted to someone of the same gender needs to know God's mercy—and his help as well—to figure out what is the healthiest, holiest way to deal with the attraction.

No one likes to realize that they have done wrong or have held the wrong beliefs. Those who humbly and courageously face it recover from shame and become happier than they ever were before. Those who hide from the truth perpetuate their shame and, in an effort to feel better about themselves, blame others.

Michael grew up in a loving, faith-filled home. But a terrible tragedy that occurred while he was in grade school began to undermine his faith and the close relationship he had with his parents.

His religious education teacher, the mother of a classmate, was a special lady. She taught the children in her home, mothering them and making sure that everyone enjoyed learning what she taught. But then, midway through the year, she was decapitated in a terrible car accident.

Death—especially when unexpected—can be a major fear-generator. For Michael, it was unnoticeable at first, but his teacher's death translated into the fear of losing his own parents.

Fast forward to Michael's high school years. In health class, he learned that people who are overweight and lead stressful lives and eat a lot of red meat are prone to heart attacks. His dad was overweight, worked in a stressful job, and loved to eat burgers and steaks. Michael asked him to change—but to no avail. Unable to control that which he feared, he diverted the energy of fear into anorexia. He couldn't stop his dad from overeating, so Michael began to under-eat.

His parents soon noticed his unhealthy behavior and took him to a therapist. Michael returned to his normal diet. However, his underlying fear of losing his father had not been uncovered.

After going off to college, Michael began to explore the occult despite hearing throughout his childhood that it's a demonic counterfeit to what God offers. The idea of gaining supernatural powers attracted him.

The promise of gaining power through occult practices is especially appealing to those who feel powerless. Occult powers are the

Devil's counterfeit of life in the Holy Spirit. When demons are given the opportunity, they pull people away from God's love.

Fear is a very common fruit of demonic invasion. Michael began to fear his parents. Even when they showed him unconditional love and gentle compassion, as soon as they were out of his sight, fear took over again.

Deep down, Michael still held within him the faith-based teachings of his childhood. He recognized that his decisions were contrary to the ways of God. But rather than face the shame that he feared, he withdrew in avoidance. And rather than discover the fear of death that motivated his fascination with the occult, he cut himself off from his parents. If any tragedy were to hit them, he wouldn't have to know about it.

But this, too, was shameful. He had to find a way to justify hiding from his parents, so he focused on bad memories from his childhood, exaggerated them, and repressed the good memories. He condemned his parents for treatment that never happened and incidents that he remembered incorrectly. (Exorcists report that one of the common signs of demonic influence is the warping of memories.)

It's a tragic story that has variations being lived out by many adult children of faith-filled, Christ-centered, church-going parents.

More than ever, people today need to learn what it means to be loved by Abba-Father. He desires to bring his unbelieving sons and daughters to Jesus, the Son he sent to Earth to die for them. How will he do it? What's his plan?

When Jesus walked the Earth, his love and mercy and compassionate concern taught—for everyone who wanted to learn the truth—that Abba-Father is real, that the Father is all-powerful, and that the Father cares. But what about today?

The good news is: Jesus is *still* here on Earth—*in us*. We are now the ones walking with the Father. We are now the ones representing the Father. We are now the ones who are called to reveal, through our behavior, what God the Father is really like. He is calling upon us to bring unbelievers to his Son. As his beloved children, we have testimonies of soul-changing miracles that need to be shared openly and often.

Today's Exercise, Part 1:
Your testimony

Take some time now to reflect on some of the amazing ways that Abba-Father has revealed himself to you. In what ways are you different than you used to be because you trust God? This is your testimony. Write it down so that it becomes easier to remember and to share. When people see how joyful and peaceful you are because you know that Abba is taking good care of you, and if you share the stories that prove it, they get the opportunity to learn what it means to be loved by the heavenly Father.

Don't continue reading until after taking note of how the Father has revealed himself to you. You'll miss out on a very necessary step if you skip this exercise.

_____

_____

_____

_____

Abba offers freedom from fear

Michael wanted to have his parents' love for many years to come, but he got caught in a trap that denied him the freedom to receive that love. It also turned him away from the perfect love of Abba-Father. That's what fear does. It steals our freedom by lying to us.

Whether a fear is small or huge, it disempowers us at the very time we're seeking to gain control. For example, the fear of not being able to find employment after being laid off from a job can pull us away from God's help by convincing us that we're failures. Fear lies to us, and so we lose the freedom to be who we truly are and to do what we're gifted and called by God to do.

Abba-Father, in contrast, freely gives us freedom: freedom from sin through Christ, and then freedom to be his adopted children—with all that this includes.

Saint John tells us in his first epistle: *"There is no fear in love. But perfect love drives out fear, because fear has to do with punishment. The one who fears is not made perfect in love"* (1 John 4:18 NIV). What are you afraid of?

When we understand what it means to be loved by Abba-Father, fear dissipates. How much anxiety we have is an indicator of how well we understand (or remember) Abba's love. To overcome anxiety, first identify the misconceptions you're believing about God, then ask the Holy Spirit to fill you with the truth about each misconception.

Remember that when we look at Jesus, we see the Father (as explained in John 14). The Father and the Son are fully united, one in being, one in purpose, one in answering our prayers. Jesus came to Earth to reveal the Father's true nature to everyone who is open to receiving his perfect love. He said, *"No one knows the Son except the Father, and no one knows the Father except the Son and those to whom the Son chooses to reveal him"* (Matthew 11:27 NIV).

Then Jesus said, *"Take my yoke upon you and learn from me"* (Matthew 11:28). Since Jesus is yoked to the Father, doing only what

Chapter 6: The Father Heals Us of Fear

he sees the Father doing, he is inviting us to be yoked to the Father *with him*. This seems burdensome if we prefer to go our own way and stay in charge of our own lives, but Jesus says, *"Surprise! This is actually the easy way to live. This is a light burden."* Why? Because when we're not pulling away from Jesus and we are cooperating with Jesus, going with him wherever he wants to go, he—not us—carries the weight of the burden.

Fear does not want us to know that the Father cares so much about us that he wants what is truly best for us. Examine the role that fear has been playing in your life. Ask yourself, "What's keeping me from fully trusting in God's goodness toward me? How does fear play into this?"

Then look at Jesus. He readily gave miracles to all who asked for help. Why? Because Abba-Father desired to provide the miracles. Jesus told us that if we have a close relationship with the Father, we will receive whatever we need.

Jesus said, *"Do not worry, saying, 'What shall we eat?' or 'What shall we drink?' or 'What shall we wear?' Your heavenly Father knows that you need them. Seek his kingdom first. Rely on him above all else. Turn to him before trying anything else. Cling to nothing but your Father, and you will be given everything you need."* (See Matthew 6:31-32.)

Fear says this is not true. Fear says that God will disappoint us.

Which voice do you believe? When you're not thinking but you're simply reacting to a problem, what do your actions and attitudes reveal about your understanding of Abba's love?

The traps of fear are rampant, but the love of the Father is always abundant.

Fear's trap #1: If you react by taking matters into your own hands, you're believing lies about God.

Defeat the fear: One good way to overcome this is to find scriptures that show God handling a bigger problem. Since he did that for those people in the Bible, he will certainly help you; after all, he gave his Son Jesus to you knowing full well that Jesus would have to suffer and die for you.

Fear's trap #2: If you entrust the problem to God and then take it back by worrying about it, fear is telling you that God can't or won't do enough good with it.

Defeat the fear: The best way to deal with this is to see yourself as God's partner in dealing with the problem. What can you do to help solve the problem? Pray about it. Convert the energy of worry into an action plan. Then sit with it for a while before acting upon it, waiting to find out if the Holy Spirit anoints the plan with divine energy. You'll know when that happens, because divine energy brings with it joy and hope and opportunities to implement the plan.

Fear's trap #3: If you repeatedly complain or lose your temper, you haven't let Abba heal your wounds. Your complaints are a cry for help. Your temper is a cry of pain.

Defeat the fear: Let God heal you through a counselor or a good friend who is solid in the Faith or through a spiritual director.

Chapter 6: The Father Heals Us of Fear

Fear's trap #4: If you're waiting for someone else to comfort you or to solve the problem by making a change, you haven't discovered that the Father's love can more than make up for what someone else is not doing.

Defeat the fear: Increase the time you spend in meaningful prayer and meditation, which will take your focus off of others and put it where it belongs.

Fear's trap #5: If you get depressed and it lasts more than a day or two, what do you wish you could control but cannot?

Defeat the fear: Ask God to reveal to you the bigger picture that he sees. "All things work together for the good of those who love the Lord" (see Romans 8:28)—so what benefits might come from the troubles you're enduring? Write down all possible answers and revisit this list whenever you need a boost in hope.

Fear's trap #6: If you know that God always walks with you during hard times but you're avoiding a person or a situation that will stir up trouble, fear is telling you that it will be irredeemably disastrous, or you will suffer unbearably.

Defeat the fear: Give God your "yes" about accepting whatever cross he knows is coming. Ask Jesus to help you carry it. Unite yourself to Jesus on his Cross by seeing the connection between what happens to you and what happened to him. By doing this, all of your sufferings will become redemptive. Praise God for the opportunity to serve him while so closely united to Jesus.

Charmaine shares how she defeats fear. She says, "When I am excessively anxious and fearful, Papa God always urges me to praise him. It's hard to keep focused in those moments, but he would not ask this of me if he knew that I could not do it. So, when I praise him consciously and from my heart, it brings the most immense peace. What I am learning is that instead of trying to desperately rid myself of the anxiety, Papa God is actually using this to draw me closer to him, to a more intimate relationship with him, while teaching me about me."

What signs of anxiety do you see in your reactions to problems? What is fear telling you? What is Abba-Father lovingly saying to you that casts out the fear?

Today's Exercise, Part 2:
Replace your fears with the Father's love

Remember that fear always lies. Think of the word "fear" (F-E-A-R) as False Evidence Appearing Real. Fear uses just enough of the truth to capture our attention and our trust, and once we trust fear, it leads us away from the truth. For example, fear tells us: "Yes, God does work miracles, but remember the miracle that you asked for and didn't get. This is proof that God is not interested in you." In this hypothesis, what feels like proof is really the *fear* that God is not interested in you.

When we don't fight the fear, it controls us and harms our relationship with the Father. The damage is automatic unless we deliberately stop the process. Since the lie that fear tells is hidden behind a truth, (as we see in the example described in the previous paragraph), we very easily—and automatically—allow the lie to control our faith and dictate our lives. And thus fear disempowers us.

This is easily cured! We need only to identify the lie that fear is telling us, renounce it in the name of Jesus, and ask the Holy Spirit (the Spirit of Truth) to reveal the truth to us. And then be still and listen.

I'll lead you through that process now.

1. Describe a fear that has been controlling your life.
_____
_____
_____

2. Next, pray from your heart, asking the Father to speak to you through his Holy Spirit.

3. Now, circle or underline the words you wrote in #1 (the description of your fear) that might possibly be a lie.

4. Pray again and listen for reasons why you, as the beloved son or daughter of the Perfect Father, do not need to be afraid.

   _____
   _____
   _____
   _____
   _____

5. Write these reasons as a love letter from the Father to you.

   _____
   _____
   _____
   _____
   _____
   _____
   _____
   _____

When you hear the truth, you will recognize it, because Jesus gave you the Holy Spirit. Is it something that helps you grow stronger in faith? Does it give you peace—but more than peace, does it bring your blood pressure down? Does it put you in touch with Abba's love? Then trust it! Then act on it.

You can add to #4 above by thumbing through the Bible and turning scriptures into a very reassuring prayer. Try this one; adapt it for your needs (for example, "though an army besiege me" might be changed to "though financial troubles besiege me"):

The Lord is my light and my salvation –
whom shall I fear?
The Lord is the stronghold of my life –
of whom shall I be afraid?

When the wicked advance against me
to devour me,
it is my enemies and my foes
who will stumble and fall.
Though an army besiege me,
my heart will not fear;
though war break out against me,
even then I will be confident.

One thing I ask from the Lord,
this only do I seek:
that I may dwell in the house of the Lord
all the days of my life,

> *to gaze on the beauty of the Lord*
> *and to seek him in his temple.*

Psalm 27:1-4 (NIV)

In other words, to overcome fears, stay in Abba's arms at all times!

7

When Doubts Tell Us God Doesn't Care

What doubts about God the Father do you have? These are undermining your faith, and today we're going to find a way to overcome them.

> *Jesus said to them, "A prophet is not without honor except in his own town and in his own home." And he did not do many miracles there because of their lack of faith. (Matthew 13:57-58 NIV)*

What if you lived in Nazareth when Jesus came into town after he had become famous for his healing and preaching ministry?

Matthew 13:54-58 shows the disbelief of people who thought they knew Jesus but their preconceptions interfered with their faith. "He's just the carpenter's son," someone said in disgust. "Who does he think he is?"

Joseph had passed away long ago, and still they describe Jesus as "the carpenter's son." Was Jesus so unnoticeable as a carpenter in his own name that he hadn't even earned a good reputation as a business owner?

Nazareth was a small town. Everyone knew each other. Why were his neighbors so surprised at his wisdom when he gave a teaching in the synagogue? Had he been just a quiet, unappealing young man before the Holy Spirit filled him at his baptism? It's hard to imagine Jesus as someone who was "just" so ordinary that no one expected greatness from him.

"And he did not do many miracles there because of their lack of faith" (verse 58).

Imagine that it's a few months prior to this scene, and you are traveling outside of Nazareth to visit a relative in Capernaum. During your visit, you hear that Jesus has been preaching on a nearby hillside. Your relatives and their friends tell you about healings they had experienced, and you see the evidence. You know they are not lying or exaggerating. So, you go to the hillside to see this Jesus for yourself, and when he teaches, you notice that he speaks with authority. You can sense love and truth behind his words.

Then you return home to Nazareth. You tell your neighbors what you had witnessed in Capernaum. But they don't believe you. In fact, they scoff at you for falling prey to superstitious nonsense.

"Don't you remember playing with Jesus when he was a little boy?" they ask. "He's no different than you and me. And remember how ordinary he was, learning the carpentry business from his father Joseph's side?"

How would their disbelief affect your beliefs? Do the doubts of others ever undermine your faith?

The influence of spiritual prejudices

So far in this book, we've been digging up the misconceptions we have about Abba-Father that originated in human failures. Now

Chapter 7: When Doubts Tell Us God Doesn't Care

let's look at preconceptions. Preconceptions originate in prejudices that we've been influenced to believe. How affected are you by spiritual prejudices?

Let's continue with our Nazareth story to find out.

Imagine that Jesus arrives in Nazareth and you rush out to see him because you're sure that he's going to work miracles like you had witnessed in Capernaum (a preconception). But nothing supernatural happens (reality has contradicted your preconception). You hear a rumor that he laid his hands on a few sick people and healed them (see Mark 6:5), but you hadn't witnessed this yourself. How do you feel about Jesus now? Did the clash between preconception and reality confuse you? Do you feel angry? Disappointed?

How do you feel now about the conversations you had when you returned home from Capernaum and told people about Jesus? Do you feel embarrassed? Belittled? Inferior? Wrong? Are you doubting yourself?

Jesus is walking down the street, passing by shops, probably on his way to the town well. It's a busy place. Will you go to Jesus and ask him for an answer to your prayers? Or will you shy away, afraid that the townspeople will scoff at you again. Do you even believe that he will give you what you ask for? Or has your confidence in him changed?

Look, there goes a crippled man who's brave enough to approach Jesus. Hope exhilarates you, because now you and your neighbors will see proof that Jesus really does do miracles! But no, what's this? The man is arguing with Jesus, and Jesus turns away from him. Jesus looks sad. Surely it's because he's unhappy about the man's condition. So, why is he walking away from him? Apparently, Jesus doesn't really care about him. This would explain why people are rejecting him.

Today, all of us have sought help from Jesus without getting it. If Jesus could walk away from a crippled man, why would he answer *your* prayers? Isn't that one of the reasons why you struggle with doubts?

The world says that Jesus is not divine. Many of those who do believe in his divinity proceed to live as if God doesn't really care. It seems like he sees our pain and walks away. The alternative is more disturbing: He sees our pain and stays, but apparently he's okay with our suffering, so he does nothing.

And if Jesus doesn't care, then neither does the Father who sent him.

We know that this is *not* right, but we struggle with it. We too readily conclude (in our hearts and in our actions if not also in our thoughts) that when our prayers are not answered, it's because God doesn't care. Or he doesn't care *enough*. Every disappointment, every long waiting, every novena and marathon of prayers reinforces that God's caring only goes so far as to say, "It's better for you if you don't get what you're asking for." He's the stern father who makes us mow the lawn in the hot sun when our friends are inviting us to go swimming in their refreshing, crystal clear pool.

Charmaine knows that it's important to balance our lives. She learned to alleviate her sufferings with laughter and singing along with songs on the radio and even dancing to the rhythm of the music. But eventually, everything became too serious. She wondered: "How do I have fun without feeling guilty, without thinking that something bad will happen after?"

Her questions are rooted in doubts about the true nature of Abba-Father. She explains: "It is so difficult for me to totally trust him, to surrender all to him. You see, I was called names as a child by my siblings and cannot remember ever being defended by either parent." Their lack of concern was reinforced by the many wrong messages of her father's alcoholism and abusiveness.

This translated into doubts about God: "I did not trust him completely. I could not believe in his goodness. Something bad must happen. I believed that he said one thing but would do another, especially when bad things would happen."

Developing a personal relationship with God has not come easy for her. She says, "By his grace I am developing one. There are lots of things I have to let go of: my pride, my will, self-righteousness, impatience, and feeling that I am running out of time and I must change *now*. I never blamed God for the things that went wrong in my life. I believed that the faults were all mine and thus I had to fix me."

We all need to work on overcoming our sinful tendencies, day by day, until the end of our earthly lives, as part of growing closer to Abba-Father. However, did you catch the contradiction in her statements of belief? This contradiction is a clue to where she needs to focus her healing.

"By God's grace, I'm developing a personal relationship with him," she said. And yet she added: "I have to fix me."

What is God's grace? It's the gift of his active intervention in our troubles. A gift! We cannot earn grace. We receive it. When we meditate on God's concern for us, we open ourselves to his grace. Our self-improvement needs to be done in partnership with Abba-Father. Our desire to be holy needs to be tied to his desire to bless us. And because of that desire, he gave us the Holy Spirit. It is the Holy Spirit who changes us (after we've given him permission to do so). He needs only our cooperation and determination to improve.

Charmaine wanted to know: "How do I have fun without feeling guilty, without thinking that something bad will happen after?" Let's look at these two common misconceptions separately.

The suspicion that something bad will always follow happy times is best handled by overcoming fear, as prescribed in the previous chapter. The fear that good times turn into bad times is common in families that have suffered abuse. If you have this fear, go back to Exercise #2 of Chapter 6 and do it again for this particular fear.

The guilty feeling that comes from having fun is cured by understanding the fun-loving nature of our Father.

Overcoming doubts

Did your human dad (or father substitute) play games with you? This question has two connotations: (1) emotional games such as "I'll reward you with my love and attention after you finish your homework, and better yet, after you get an A+ on the exam," and (2) fun games such as sports, cards, board games, video games, and swimming in a refreshing, crystal clear pool.

Trust is built when people play fun games together. The camaraderie of it forges a bond like nothing else can.

For our trust in Abba-Father to deepen, we need to discover that he knows how to have fun. He's the Daddy who says the lawn can

Chapter 7: When Doubts Tell Us God Doesn't Care

wait and then he drives us to the swimming pool and splashes in the water with us.

Have you noticed the activities of this fun-loving God in your life?

It's an accurate image of God the Father. Who do you think invented fun? God, of course! He designed his children to have a playful spirit.

One of my favorite activities for relaxation and restoration is boating. When the dolphins play—and they definitely have a spirit of fun—alongside our boat, it's a gift from Abba's playfulness. When the seagulls follow us, gliding on the air above the wake behind the boat, they're hungry and they're watching for lunch to splash up from the churned water. And it's fun to watch. Abba called those birds over to our boat.

When we owned our own boat, Ralph often joked that, when we're on the water, I'm a storm magnet. We've been caught in the rain and thunder and lightning too many times, but God has always kept us safe.

It's an exciting adventure when you know that you're doing it with a fun-loving Abba.

One of my favorite memories is only a favorite because of how funny it was. We were boating on the far side of Tampa Bay near our home in Florida. The peaceful weather suddenly turned into a severe storm. The squall line between us and home port was too dangerous to pass through, so we headed for the nearest dock to ride out the winds and torrential rains in safety.

However, the dock belonged to a wealthy man who came running up to us, getting drenched by the rain. He was worried, I guess, that we were going to damage his dock. After we showed him how well we had secured the lines, he invited us to come into his house. *Wow, how hospitable!* we thought. As it turned out, he only wanted to keep a close eye on us. He ushered us into a room directly off his patio. He gave us a couple of towels, turned the television on to a continual weather report, and sat there quietly watching it as we waited for the storm to pass. I thought it was hilarious that he should think that Ralph and I might be thieves.

Since he was not interested in conversation, he never learned what kind of people we really are. He remained clueless about us, but God knew us and God still laughs with me whenever I think about this story.

Today's Exercise, Part 1:
Laugh

Charmaine discovered that Father God "has the heartiest, most robust laugh ever." When he rejoices, he *really* rejoices!

What funny stories do you have from your own life? Write down a few words that identify each incident (for example, "the rich man's dock incident"). Where is God in these stories? Identify his presence in them and then imagine the two of you laughing together.

_____
_____
_____
_____

_____

_____

_____

_____

Abba wants to relieve your suffering

God designed us to enjoy life. A corollary truth is: He designed us to understand that relief from suffering is important. This is who he is. He is a healer, not a destroyer. He is no sadist. He enjoys life and he enjoys sharing his joy with us. While it's true that Jesus spoke about carrying crosses, and it's true that our agonies unite us to Jesus, and it's true that hardships can lead to important lessons and purifications, Father God does not enjoy watching us suffer. He rejoices when our pain is healed.

For many years I suffered the rejection of someone who is very important to me. I lifted him up to the Lord every day during my morning prayers. In church, I offered up the Mass for him and prayed for our reconciliation. Countless friends prayed the Rosary for him and remembered us in their daily prayers. We all knew that God was bigger than the problems that divided us. And yet, two decades passed and the rejection remained as deep and divisive as ever.

Sometimes I wondered if all those prayers made any difference: What would happen if I stopped interceding for him? But the pain in my heart wouldn't let me quit. Daily this precious soul needed to be lifted up to the Lord, so I faithfully continued to pray and hope and wait and endure the pain of rejection.

One year on his birthday, I asked God to give me a sign that the prayers made a difference. Immediately, Abba, my Divine Doting Daddy, began to minister to me. He didn't reassure me that the end of the suffering would soon come, though I had very much hoped he would. But he did relieve my suffering by filling me with an awareness of how dear I am to him. He reassured me of his love for me (even though I was not doubting this). And he let me know that he appreciates my sacrifice.

You see, at the root of the rejection was my passion for serving the Lord. The Devil hates me and wishes to retaliate against my ministry. Because he could not stop me from making a difference for the Kingdom of God, he found an opportunity to hurt me through the rejection of a loved one. For a season I even heard the whispered lie, "If you shut down Good News Ministries, I will release my hold on this person." Of course, this only drove me to serve the Lord with more passion.

The passion to remain in Christ does not remove the sting of being rejected. But Abba-Father compensates for that. Whatever the cause of your suffering, remember this: The Father is doting on you. He is right now reassuring you of his unrelenting love. He is appreciating the sacrifices you have made.

However, it can be difficult to feel God's appreciation. This is not because he's ignoring us. It's because we don't believe it. Where does this doubt come from?

Sometimes it comes from our misunderstandings about humility and pride. It's prideful to think about how wonderful we are, right? But Abba-Father is telling you *right now* what is wonderful about you. Can you hear him? Or is "humility" interfering?

True humility recognizes that God knows us so well that he even knows what is wonderful about us. True humility recognizes that our wonderfulness comes from God himself. We were made in his image. Jesus gave us the Holy Spirit to empower us to grow in holiness and overcome the sins that hide our wonderfulness. True humility accepts these truths as we rely on his help.

What else causes you to doubt? Disbelief in the goodness of God? How about someone else's disbelief in your goodness? Let neither self-focus nor self-abasement keep you from receiving and enjoying the appreciation that God is beaming at you. Abba-Daddy wants to reassure us that he cares very much about how we feel.

Today's Exercise, Part 2:
Be reassured that God cares about your concerns

Abba-Father designed us to enjoy doing works that serve as an outlet for the gifts and talents he's given us. Are you fulfilled in your work? He also designed into us the desire to earn enough to take good care of our families. If we have financial problems, it's not because God doesn't care. Perhaps he's teaching us to get our priorities right. Have we purchased more than we should because the world has made it seem good to keep buying new, bigger, and better? Or perhaps it's the injustices of others that have caused our problems. Have we forgiven them? And have we asked Abba-Father to show us the hidden blessings that he has provided?

What are the unanswered prayers you have? What are you concerned about? Take time now to list the biggest concerns you have. Then think about: "Why am I so concerned about these?"

_____

_____

_____

_____

_____

_____

_____

_____

_____

_____

Next, focus on this answer: "Because I care." Where do you think this concern came from? God, of course! When we care about others and we want to see a problem get resolved, we are sharing in God's true nature.

Since this is how God designed you, of course he wants to make a difference in everything that you're concerned about. Your loving concern is union with his compassion. This union is itself a form of prayer. In fact, it's a mutual communication of what God wants to do.

Can we care *too much* and maybe even get in the way of God's work? In truth, there is no such thing as caring "too much." Ask this: Is it possible for God to care too much? I've never heard anyone complain that he cares too much. If we care so much that it hurts, we are joining Jesus in his Passion when he cared so much that he suffered excruciating pain and died for us.

Yes, caring "too much" can get in the way of God's work, but only if we take matters into our own hands in order to stop the suffering of our passion. Or if we reject the relief that God offers because we want things to turn out differently.

He wants to answer all of our prayers and relieve all of our concerns, but usually not as fast as we want him to. He waits on the free will cooperation of everyone who's involved. He wants the best for everyone. So, he's already working a plan (a plan for good, not disaster—see Jeremiah 29:11) and in the meantime he's already doing more than we can ask for or imagine (see Ephesians 3:20). A good prayer life with quiet meditation time makes it clear what this "more" is while we wait.

What have you learned while waiting? What blessings have come from the wait? What have you become stronger in? And what about those who have been delaying God's plan? What have they become stronger in?

Today's Exercise, Part 3:
Finding proof that God cares

Next, take the list of your concerns, which you wrote about in part 2 of today's exercise. This time rewrite them into sentences thanking God for being concerned. Use the following sentence-starter, replacing the name "Abba-Father" with whichever name for him that you like:

Thank you, Abba-Father, for being concerned about
_____.

Thank you, Abba-Father, for being concerned about
_____.

Thank you, Abba-Father, for being concerned about
_____.

Thank you, Abba-Father, for being concerned about
_____.

Thank you, Abba-Father, for being concerned about
_____.

Thank you, Abba-Father, for being concerned about
_____.

Thank you, Abba-Father, for being concerned about
_____.

Thank you, Abba-Father, for being concerned about
_____.

Thank you, Abba-Father, for being concerned about
_____.

The importance of good friends who have strong faith

Most of us live in Nazareth. Our whole society is Nazareth. To fully believe that Jesus is showing us that Abba-Father cares, we need to find other faith-filled believers and spend a lot of time with them. To have unquestionable trust in Abba's helpfulness, we need to gather with them in prayer groups and volunteer work and social get-togethers.

Let's return to Capernaum. This time, imagine that you're with Jairus, the synagogue leader. His daughter has just died, but Jesus tells him, "Don't be afraid; just believe! She will be healed."

When you and Jairus arrive with Jesus at his house, Jesus chases out the neighbors and relatives who are wailing and mourning. Notice how he reacts to their scoffing. "Stop wailing," Jesus tells them. "She is not dead but asleep." Of course, they don't believe him. They mock him. Everyone knows the girl is cold dead.

Jesus does not let anyone enter into the house with him except Peter, John and James, and Jairus and his wife, and *you*. After Jesus closes the door and the disbelievers are shut out, you look hopefully at this amazingly confident man. You cannot hear the wailing anymore. You can only hear the breathing of each person in the room. Nothing is distracting you from noticing the love on the face of Jesus. And the peace. And his tender smile as he reaches for the dead girl's hand and says, "My child, get up!"

She stirs. Her spirit returns to her body, and she pops up off the bed. She glances quickly at the strangers and announces to her parents, *"What's there to eat around here? I'm starving."* (See Luke 8:40-56.)

To stop doubting that Abba-Father cares about your concerns, we need to leave Nazareth, pass through Capernaum, and move to Bethany. Here is where the closest friends of Jesus will become our friends. Bethany is where Jesus raised one of his friends from the dead.

Bethany can be any of the "hot spots" around the globe where miracles are common. Hot spots are locations where the Holy Spirit's fire is vibrantly active because whole communities of believers meet regularly to feed their faith and help each other overcome doubts. Join them online if that's the only way you can do it. In person is better.

The larger the group of faith-filled believers that surround us, the easier it is to feel the presence of Abba-Father ministering to us, speaking to us, and embracing us. Hopefully your church community is full of believers who are alive in the faith. Worshiping with them should be an experience that makes connecting to God a supernatural reality. This is the way God designed church to be—read the Book of Acts.

Unfortunately, in-person, Spirit-filled prayer groups are not always possible.

What do we do then? How do we reach the level of faith where we know, always and under all circumstances, that Abba-Father cares?

We can travel to Bethany spiritually. It's important that we seek out friends who want the same level of faith or have already achieved it. We create a Bethany with them. The worldly people we associate with will drag us down and take our eyes off of God. They are incapable of strengthening our faith. The same is true for Christians who are weak and disinterested in faith growth. However, finding our Bethany friends and building good relationships with them will require giving up personal agendas and normal activities if they interfere with spending time with our Bethany friends. This is not easy, but it's a lot easier than trying to reach higher levels of faith by ourselves.

In the experiences of Bethany friendships, our confidence grows. Doubts give way to increased trust. Insecurities about Abba's love disappear under the compassionate guidance of friends who have already overcome similar doubts.

Meanwhile, there *is* something very helpful that you can do alone. Pray:

Holy Spirit, teach me the truth.
Lord Jesus, deliver me from the doubts and false teachings of the world.
Abba-Father, I cannot escape from them on my own. Carry me.

8

Dealing with Disappointment

Rarely are our prayers answered instantly. And there are good reasons for this. Divine reasons. If we could see it from God's perspective, we'd be grateful for the journey of waiting. But our first instinct is to see it from our own limited perspective. And this leads to disappointment.

> *Yet those who wait for the* Lord */ Will gain new strength; / They will mount up with wings like eagles, / They will run and not get tired, / They will walk and not become weary. (Isaiah 40:31 NASB)*

When I was 17, one of my favorite rock stars performed in a small, nearby city. This was an opportunity I did not want to miss. Afraid that my parents would forbid it, a friend and I bought tickets and arranged transportation. I reasoned that if I had already spent my money for it, surely my parents wouldn't stop me from going.

They did.

I cried. I cajoled. I explained that the tickets were not refundable, that my friend was allowed to go but only if she had a companion, and that I was mature enough now to handle a rock concert without getting into drugs or anything else bad that they thought might happen at the concert.

None of this mattered. The answer was still "NO."

Although they were rightfully protecting me, I didn't see it that way at the time. I felt old enough and mature enough and safe enough to go to a rock concert without an adult. It took me a long time to forgive them for that.

We do the same thing with God. Even when we get older and more mature, our hearts can get so fixated on a goal that sometimes we try to trick God into saying yes. Oh, we probably don't think of it as tricking him. We know that this would be wrong. But if we assume that the only way to get what we want is to plan it ourselves, spend time and money on it, and *then* pray about it, we're definitely trying to trick him (however unconscious this might be).

Have you ever prayed something like this *after* starting a new venture? "Oh Lord, look at the good this is doing already. You know this project is a blessing to others. But I need Your extra help now. I can't see any reason why You wouldn't want me to continue doing this, especially if You help me get it done." Did you forget to seek the Holy Spirit's guidance *before* you got started?

First we make up our minds about what we think is best, and then we ask the Lord to help us do what we've already decided is right. I've seen this trick used to justify getting divorced. I know people who've had abortions this way.

It's manipulative, and God won't be manipulated. And self-made agendas are always inferior to God's plans, no matter how sensible they seem.

Sometimes we try to manipulate the *truth*. For example: "I know I'm supposed to get married instead of living with my sweetheart, but we really do love each other, and if it's loving, it can't be sinful." But truth is unchangeable, no matter how we try to change it. Sin is destructive, no matter how we try to justify it. Including when we sin in the name of love.

Underneath the self-justification and the manipulation are the desire to be in control instead of surrendering to God, the hope of avoiding disappointment, and the prideful fear of being wrong. Ironically, in trying to get what we want outside of God's will, inevitably we get into situations that we cannot control, we end up disappointed, and we suffer from wasted time and money or some other valued commodity. And in the process, our understanding of the Father's protective love gets lost or damaged.

Even after we've matured beyond trying to manipulate God, disappointments from the past might still be affecting our relationship with Abba-Father today. To find out, ask yourself: "Am I expecting to be disappointed in my prayer requests? Or do I trust Abba-Father so much that I'm actually pleased when he says 'no' or 'not yet' to my ideas?"

The Spiritual Success Principle

God answers prayers in one of three ways: "Yes," "Not right now," or "I have something better in mind." When we trust God, we gladly accept any answer he gives to us. But how do we know what his answer is? First, we need to have a personal relationship with the Holy Spirit because the Father gave us the Holy Spirit to be our Helper and Teacher. When our souls are submitted to the Holy Spirit, we become able to recognize the voice of God. In addition to this, we also need friends or a spiritual director who can help us know when guidance from the Father is not just something we conjured up. (We all have the human desire to fill in the blanks of God's messages when we don't hear him well. This is us being in control. This is us trying to manipulate the situation.)

Jeanie describes how she hears God's answer to her prayer requests: "I wait either for my request to be granted at a later date or for him to answer it in a totally different way. It amazes me what happens. The answer is something I never expected. Sometimes he changed the circumstances so that the problem was eliminated, and sometimes he took me out of the situation without me having to do anything."

Waiting on God for guidance can seem tricky. It's so easy to mess it up. How should we do it? How do we wait without fear and anxiety but with faith and hope?

I'm the kind of person who doesn't like to sit still while waiting on God to direct me. I go knocking on doors, so to speak, to find out which opportunity God will open. This works successfully, but it usually involves wasted time while I stand in front of doors that never open. The Holy Spirit has been teaching me a better way: Think about it all you want, pray to receive clarity, and move forward when circumstances fall into place. Meanwhile, stay busy with what you already have in your life and enjoy it.

That is the Spiritual Success Principle.

Knocking on doors (looking for opportunities to fulfill your dream or reach your objective) does work as long as you don't knock so hard that you break the door down. Or get bruised knuckles.

When circumstances begin to fall into place, we often wonder, "Is this just a coincidence? Am I reading too much into it? I need more confirmation from God before I can act on this." The desire for confirmation is a holy one but it can also turn us into procrastinators. Again, talking it over with a good friend who is mature in faith or a spiritual director is often necessary. But in the end, the decision is yours. It's another lesson in trusting God. Whenever you think that God might be telling you to do something, go ahead and move forward with it while asking God to redirect you if you're misunderstanding his will.

My prayer for this is: "Father God, it seems like it's a good idea to ___. It seems like it meets with Your approval. Therefore, I'm going to act on it, but please, if ever I go in the wrong direction, grab me by the ankles so I cannot move forward without tripping. Then turn me toward the direction You want me to go."

This is another way to apply the Spiritual Success Principle. It always works, but at the moment of tripping, we might conclude that God is failing us. Fiona felt sure that God wanted her to have a job that opened up because "everything seemed to be falling into place perfectly."

"But," she bemoaned, "humiliation and failure were lined up for me instead. It wasn't as though I wanted the job in the first place. My judgement wasn't clouded by my own agenda or enthusiasm. The way things were happening, everything seemed to indicate that it was God's will that I should go for it. I honestly don't care that I did not get the job. I was disappointed because I thought that the Lord was showing me that he was leading me to a new phase in my walk with him—one where he would lead and I would know that he was nudging me in one direction or another and I would be given the grace to follow."

One of the clues that we are following God's plan is the passion we feel about it. Psalm 37:4 tells us to *"Take delight in the LORD, and he will give you the desires of your heart"* (NIV). This doesn't mean that he *fulfills* the desires of our heart as if he were a magic genie making our wishes come true. It means that he *places within us* the desires that he plans to fulfill. What do you feel passionate about? Where do you think that passion came from? Something in your circumstances triggered it but it originated in the passionate heart of the Father.

If everything falls into place but you don't feel a passionate desire to do it, like what happened to Fiona, don't move forward in it until you examine *why* you don't have a desire for it. Submit yourself to the Father. Surrender to him your lack of desire. Then ask the Holy Spirit to set you on fire with a passion for it, if it is the Father's will. If you've truly surrendered all of your reasons for not wanting to do it, it won't be long before a supernatural passion for it wells up within you.

Jason discovered the Spiritual Success Principle when he applied for college. He had worked very hard during high school in order to pursue aerospace engineering. His scores were high, he took Advanced Placement courses, and he participated in clubs and sports. And with God on his side, even though there were a lot of students applying to the same university, he felt sure that he'd get in.

He waited eagerly for his letter of acceptance to arrive. When it finally did, he opened it confidently, ready to get on with celebrating his admission acceptance. But it was a rejection.

Three fellow students were accepted. Jason knew for a fact that their grades and SAT scores were not as good as his. Did the admis-

Chapter 8: Dealing with Disappointment

sions department make a mistake? Did God? Jason was so disappointed and shocked that he called to ask if an error had been made. He was told that there were many good candidates, and they tried to vary which ones they accepted. He was then told to keep up his grades at whatever college he chose and then reapply for the second semester. A number of students would drop out in the first semester and, due to his excellent record, he should have no problem getting in at that time. The admissions director even told Jason to contact him personally.

So, off he went to another college and kept up his hard work. As the semester progressed, he decided not to reapply to his first choice, because this other college had a much higher-rated aerospace program and he had great professors who were mentoring him well. He was very happy there and realized that this is where Father God had placed him. It was such a good fit!

God is so good and so caring that he does the same type of intervention for those who are not advanced enough in faith yet to think about asking him for help. Charmaine did not have the kind of relationship she has now with the Father when she traveled into the United States to help a friend. She decided, without prayer, to apply for a six-month visa.

"We both expected Immigration to allow me a six-month stay, as was the usual. I was given three." She felt disappointed but, "As it turned out, because of personality differences, I was more than happy to return home after the three months."

While she was packing to fly to the U.S., the Holy Spirit told her not to take along her gold jewelry. But she dismissed the message as just her own imagination. In less than a month they were stolen.

Even this became a blessing in Abba-Father's loving hands. "I know now," she says, "that I was being stripped of worldly attachments." Detachment from worldly goods enables us to become more attached to God. This too is an example of the Spiritual Success Principle.

Today's Exercise, Part 1:
Disappointment

Think of a time when you felt disappointed by God. Write the story of what happened.

_____
_____
_____
_____
_____
_____
_____
_____
_____
_____

Every child experiences the disappointment of wanting something, wishing for it with all their heart, and not getting it. We learn disappointment at a very young age. The baby who is hungry and not immediately fed experiences disappointment. The toddler who cries to be held and is ignored by well-meaning but busy and distracted parents experiences disappointment and, deep down, never forgets.

When my children were growing up, Ralph and I believed that it's important and holy to sacrifice the income of one of the parents (me) to raise the children and be there for them when they are not in school. When our finances got frighteningly tight and the children were old enough to mind themselves for a couple of hours after school, I took a job as a staff writer for my diocese's weekly newspaper. But when David and Tammy's grades began to slip and we noticed other clues revealing that my absence was making a difference, I quit the job. Knowing that God wanted me give more attention to my children, I asked God to honor my obedience by helping us pay the bills—and he did, somehow, of course.

I took up freelance writing, giving me lots of time to spend with the kids. The rule was: If Mom is working at her typewriter (or later, her computer) and you need her attention, respect her needs, and wait. She will get back to you shortly.

But David didn't understand it that way. He didn't want to wait, so he felt rejected and neglected. Even though he soon got the attention he sought, what he remembered later was the rejection.

In our relationship with God, we feel the same child-to-parent disappointment. Every prayer that goes unanswered the way we want it to and as fast as we want it to reinforces the experience of rejection, neglect, and disappointment. Even though we know that God has a better plan, the feelings of rejection and disappointment can sneak up on us and undermine our closeness to Abba.

In the heat of the moment, frustration takes over. We're tired of dealing with problems that we had hoped God would miraculously fix by now. This feeling makes it easy to forget the promises of God. We forget the miracles that happened in the past. We forget the blessing-filled attention that he gave us. If we could shut out the disappointment to recall previous times of his divine intervention, our faith and our patience would get a boost.

Parents disappoint their children usually because they understand something that the children do not. Perhaps a child keeps begging to go on an expensive vacation to Disney World and you know that the family cannot afford it. How do you feel? You want to give it to your child; you want to see all of your children happily enjoying the sights and sounds and rides of Disney entertainment. But you know that it would mean sacrificing their enrollment in Catholic school or some other benefit that's more valuable than enjoying a few days of entertainment.

In our relationship with Abba-Father, it's healing to remember that God knows more and understands more than we do about whatever it is we are wishing for, dreaming of, and hoping for. He always wants what is best for us. And, like we do when we have to disappoint our own children, he feels the disappointment with us. Like every good parent, our Heavenly Daddy wants to see us enjoying the sights and sounds of a well-lived earthly life.

The difference between hoping and wishing

When you experience the kind of disappointments that come with suffering, do you get angry at God? This anger means that you believe in him and trust him, and you're surprised that he has apparently let you down. It means that you feel close enough to him to hope for a good outcome.

Hope is not wishful thinking. It's the awareness of God's goodness and expecting to be able to enjoy that goodness. Hope means celebrating what is certainly going to happen before it happens. This certainty comes from realizing the bigger picture, i.e., the biggest picture of all: The Father sent the Son to us so that we can get to Heaven and spend eternity with him, and he gave us the Holy Spirit to help us while we're still on Earth. In other words, the Father cares so much about us that he gives us everything we need to experience his goodness forever.

Daddy-God is telling you, "Look! I am bigger than any and all of the problems you're suffering!"

He cares about you more than anyone else ever could. He cares about everything that's bothering you, even you more than you do yourself. He is infinitely more powerful and more insightful and cleverer than you are. And he has a much better idea of how to resolve your problems.

There's always great reason to hope!

Psalm 23:1-6 (NIV) reinforces this:

> *The Lord is my shepherd, I lack nothing.*
> *He makes me lie down in green pastures,*

> *he leads me beside quiet waters,*
> *he refreshes my soul....*
> *Even though I walk*
> *through the darkest valley,*
> *I will fear no evil,*
> *for you are with me;*
> *your rod and your staff,*
> *they comfort me....*
> *Surely your goodness and love will follow me*
> *all the days of my life,*
> *and I will dwell in the house of the Lord*
> *forever.*

We often think of Jesus as the Good Shepherd, but remember that King David wrote this beautiful psalm long before Jesus was born. He wrote it about God the Father. Like David, we can trust the Father because he is greater than any evils we endure. He brings light into darkness, protects us in battle, and provides rest in our exhaustion.

To "dwell in the house of the Lord forever" means that, because of his love for us and our love for him, we remain in him every moment; he sanctifies every moment, engulfing every situation with his mighty presence.

Hope is the fruit of trusting in God's love. To say, "I hope he will help me" is to say, "Of course he will help me, but I can't see the proof of it yet."

Hope involves waiting. Hope is telling you that God has already answered your prayers. He began to act the moment you turned to him for help. He even planned what to do about it before you knew you had a problem!

Hope is what enables us to have peace while we wait to see the results. Hope enables us to have patience while we wait on God's perfect timing, remembering that he cares about us *and* everyone else who's involved.

Wishful thinking, on the other hand, is hoping without faith. Hope requires faith. Our hope for answered prayers is based on who God is and what his ultimate plans are and our desire to be in those plans. We cannot see the future, but we trust the One who does see the future. As Saint Paul said in Romans 8:24, "Hope that is seen is no hope at all. Who hopes for what they already have?"

To increase your hope, spend time reflecting on all the reasons why you can trust God. Go back to the second column in the Box of Differentiation that you wrote for Chapter 2. You will discover that you have more than enough hope to endure your current problems while God works his grand plan. Meditating on this will give you the healing and peace that will strengthen you for the journey of waiting.

Hope produces joy. If your feeling of disappointment has not yet been converted into joy, ask for the supernatural help of the Holy Spirit.

May the God of hope fill you with all joy and peace as you trust in him, so that you may overflow with hope by the power of the Holy Spirit. (Romans 15:13 NIV)

What have you longed for in prayer? Even if that prayer is never answered in your lifetime, what's your reason for continuing to hope? In the answer to that lies a healthy, happy relationship with Abba-Father. It's where you're sitting on his lap and feeling loved and protected.

Abba never stops doing good for us

Our Divine Father is always helping us. He is always doing good to us and for us. But unless we can see it during times of trial and stress, it's easy to doubt it.

When bad things happen, do you sometimes wonder: "Where is God?" Don't trust your feelings. Trust God. Your feelings will tell you, "God has abandoned you." Feelings change; God and his love for you never change. Love is not love unless love is given. Because God *is* love, it's utterly impossible for him to withdraw his loving presence from you.

For I am convinced that neither death nor life, neither angels nor demons, neither the present nor the future, nor any powers, neither height nor depth, nor anything else in all creation, will be able to separate us from the love of God that is in Christ Jesus our Lord. (Romans 8:38-39 NIV)

God is actively using your trials to refine and define you. Trust him. Let him turn bad into good.

And we know that in all things God works for the good of those who love him, who have been called according to his purpose. (Romans 8:28 NIV)

Chapter 8: Dealing with Disappointment

God also intends that what you gain from your trials will influence and change the lives of others. It's never only about us. The good that God does for us is not much good unless he multiplies it through us. Often he turns our experiences into a ministry that influences others. It might be a parish ministry, it might be an online ministry, it might be something huge, or it might be a personal ministry of using your gifts and talents with your next-door neighbor. But the help that God gives through answered prayer is never intended to benefit just one person.

Don't try to hurry the process of turning bad into good; you'll only get frustrated because you can't speed up the process, no matter how you try. Remember what happened to Joseph in the Old Testament (starting with Genesis 37). After his brothers dropped him into the depths of a pit to get rid of him, there was nothing he could do about it. He couldn't climb out, jump out, levitate out, or talk his way out. All he could do was pray and wait upon the Lord.

What happened next might not have seemed like the answer to his prayers: He was sold into slavery. But in the long run (20-plus years), God's plan was awesome. Joseph endured a lot, including unjust imprisonment, until finally he was made the Pharaoh's overseer, in charge of the whole land of Egypt. It would be another nine years until his brothers came to him seeking food because of a famine. (Joseph had wisely ordered the storing of extra food supplies during the years of good crops.) Thus, he became a sort of messiah for the Hebrew people.

Joseph learned a lot during those three decades. He grew spiritually mature. God endowed him with mystical gifts (the interpretation of dreams). Likewise, as we wait for our prayers to be answered, we need to be alert to new revelations. God always offers us amazing new discoveries. Suffering usually is rewarded with mystical gifts. These wonderful blessings are the first installments of the good that the Father pulls from bad experiences.

One day when I was begging God to take action in a problem that seemed unending, he increased my faith (and patience) by inspiring me to look at the empty air in the room around me. The air was not really empty. Molecules of oxygen filled the space around me, as well as dust and human skin cells and dog dander and pollen from outdoors.

More than that, the air was filled with God himself. Suddenly I realized that everything around us is always "pregnant" with God's activity. Like the air, we are surrounded by Abba's goodness. Like me in my prayer chair, we are living *in* his helpfulness. Like a pregnancy, growth occurs while we wait. God's plans are unseen for a while, but they are nonetheless under development.

I think one of the most disappointing verses in scripture is John 14:13. Jesus said, "I will do whatever you ask when you pray in My name, so that the Father may be glorified in the Son." *Whatever?* How many times have you seen this *not* answered? I feel the sting of unanswered prayers every day.

"Come on, Jesus. You promised! Let's glorify the Father!"

Nothing changes. More disappointment.

We need new eyes.

My friend Elyse, a long-time member of my prayer support team, often tells me, "God always answers your prayers, Terry." Really? Whenever she says that, I wonder what she sees that I don't.

Remember what I said earlier in this chapter about the importance of having friends? Elyse is an example of that for me. When I asked her to cover in prayer a very long and difficult problem, she not only prayed for that, she also prayed for words that could lift my spirit.

She said, "Waiting on the Lord is hard to do, but his timing is always amazing to me. He certainly knows the desires of your heart. So, it's ok to release the dream into his hands, which I know you have done, and see what happens. You, dear sister, have been on an incredible and exciting journey. Of course, there have been obstacles, disappointments, dreams dashed. But look at all the wonderful things God is accomplishing through your obedience and determination. His Holy Spirit is alive and well in you!"

I never saw it that way before. God had probably tried to tell me this directly, but I didn't hear him until Elyse spoke it. I couldn't see what God was doing in my long stretch of waiting until I saw it through her eyes.

Disappointment happens when our eyes remain fixated on our goals, our dreams, or our desires. Joy happens when we put our focus back on the Lord and learn to look at each situation through his eyes. This life (this pre-Heaven pilgrimage) will always have obstacles, disappointments, and dashed dreams—even when we stay completely within God's plans, pursuing goals that he inspired. The important thing is not what is disappointing but what God is accomplishing despite the disappointments.

Blessed are those whose strength is in you,
whose hearts are set on pilgrimage.

> *As they pass through the Valley of Baka,*
> *they make it a place of springs;*
> *the autumn rains also cover it with pools.*
> *They go from strength to strength,*
> *till each appears before God in Zion.*
>
> *(Psalm 84:5-7 NIV)*

These verses describe a spiritual law that affects everyone in the Kingdom of God: We pass through the Valley of Baka on the way to greatness. The Hebrew word *bakah* means "to weep, to bemoan."

Abba-Father will produce greatness from every situation that we turn over to him. We can choose to live in this greatness (which exists even before we see it), for this is where we experience his tremendous love for us. Or we can live in continual disappointment, which is a nasty-smelling waft from the pits of Hell, deteriorating our friendship with the Father. It's Satan who wants us to be disappointed, not God.

St. Augustine summed it up well: "Our Father: at this name love is aroused in us…and the confidence of obtaining what we are about to ask. …What would he not give to his children who ask, since he has already granted them the gift of being his children?"

Overcoming obstacles

There are a myriad of reasons why good goals and holy desires meet with delays and obstacles. Some have to do with the wrong decisions we have made. Some have to do with the sins of others. Some happen because we live in an imperfect world; we're not in Heaven yet. Some occur because the Earth is a battlefield with demons fighting against the good that God has planned. And some are part of God's overarching plan.

I hate delays and obstacles. When Ralph and I built our house in 2012, we suffered from so many permit and construction delays that completing the project seemed impossible. We had to seriously discern which of the above-mentioned reasons for the delays we were dealing with. Had we made a wrong decision in starting the project? The stress was enormous. The problems were potentially disastrous financially.

Our Good Father had foreknown what would happen. In his great love for us, he gave clear signs at the very beginning that the decision was good and that all would end up well. One such sign was the unlikely event of both the land surveyor and the scientist from the Environmental Protection Agency showing up at the same time. The property's owner gave us only two weeks to investigate whether or not to purchase the land. Our builder informed us that the EPA would take a month to get out there. But when the scientist showed up at the same time as the land surveyor, which made the scientist's job easier, Ralph and I knew that God's hand was in it. Remembering this is what gave us the courage to persevere with hope during every delay and obstacle.

Here is one very valuable lesson that I learned from the experience; I pass it on to you to multiply the blessing: An obstacle is just a temporary problem seeking God's solution.

The good of waiting

Nearly every answered prayer requires waiting. Disappointment comes from expecting the wait to be as short as we wish it could be.

We're always waiting for something, right? Life is full of one wait after another and multiple waits simultaneously. Waiting feels like a bad thing, because we wait with impatience. Impatience comes from the worry that our worst fears might be realized or that disappointment will be the end result or that when good does happen, it won't be good enough.

Another problem with waiting, for many people, is the tendency to blame ourselves for the delay or (worse) for never getting the help that's needed. The reasoning goes like this: God is good, so if my prayers are still not answered, it's because I'm the one who is not good. I shouldn't feel disappointed in God because the delay is my fault. I have disappointed God by being not good enough. The bad situations are the result of making a bad decision or they are a punishment for my past laziness or sins.

Stop that train of thought! This is Satan accusing you. He wants you to feel discouraged and, at the same time, keep your focus on yourself instead of God. The truth is: Even if you committed the worse sin in the world, if you repented of it, God is not blinded by it. If you pray with a spirit of love and with good (holy) motivations, you are praying like a saint.

As Charmaine's story illustrates, we don't have to be perfect to receive God's help. (It's impossible anyway, so why let the Devil trick you into feeling bad about your imperfections?) God's responsiveness to your prayer requests is not controlled by your decisions and your behaviors. God's helpfulness is not dictated by how good you are.

Love is not love if it's not actively loving you, and because God is love, it's utterly impossible for him to withhold from you the answer to your prayers. Unanswered prayers are not dead prayers. Unanswered prayers are not evidence that God doesn't care (although the Devil wants you to think he's uncaring). Unanswered prayers are merely answered prayers still waiting for time to catch up to reality. The reality is: God began working on a plan for many blessings to result from your prayer request before you even began to pray about it, and he will surely see it through to completion. In the meantime, you're only waiting for time to catch up to this reality.

The belief that waiting is bad is a misconception. Waiting is actually a good thing! Even Heaven waits. This seems odd because, in eternity, time as we know it is meaningless. In eternity, all is "now." And yet, those who have gone there before us are waiting for the time when we will join them. Saints pray for us and wait with us for the fruits of their prayers.

Since everything in Heaven is good, waiting must be good.

"The Lord is not slow in keeping his promise, as some understand slowness. Instead he is patient with you, not wanting anyone to perish, but everyone to come to repentance." (2 Peter 3:9 NIV)

The author of this verse was referring to the promised Second Coming of Christ, but we can learn from it an important principle about waiting: In every promise that God has made, waiting is always beneficial. More people will benefit. More lessons will be learned. More blessings will be given to us during the wait.

Abba-Father gives us the Holy Spirit to teach us how to overcome the obstacles and to guide us to the goal. Wallowing in disappointment and all the negative feelings that come with it only paralyzes us. Relying on the Holy Spirit makes even the biggest of (divinely inspired) dreams come true in Abba's perfect timing.

When Ralph and I built our house, we knew it wasn't God who put up the obstacles. Since we had seen the Father's loving hand in the start of the project, we pushed forward and, with inspired guidance from the Holy Spirit, found our way around and over every obstacle. In October of 2012, we moved into our new home. Two weeks later, my parents moved into it, too, so that we could become their caregivers.

As it turned out, some of the obstacles were blessings in disguise, because they forced us to change some of the original design plans. The changes created a better environment for sharing the house with my parents. Abba-Father had taken our house plans and adapted them without waiting for us to ask him to do it. He knew that we didn't have the foresight to ask.

Today's Exercise, Part 2:
Blessings

Revisit what you wrote in Part 1 of today's exercise. Look again at your description of a time when you felt disappointed by God. Next, name some of the blessings that came from that trial.

Abba-Father is so caring!

_____
_____
_____
_____

Chapter 8: Dealing with Disappointment

9

The Discipline of Abba-Father

In this day of our journey deeper and deeper into the Father's Heart, let's look at how much we're influenced by the fear of punishment. Does the discipline of a good father always mean punishment? Could it be that we wrongly interpret the pain of discipline as a bad thing?

Do we want to hide from God when he disciplines us? Or do we run to him with thanksgiving because he has taught us something valuable?

> *Endure hardship as discipline; God is treating you as his children. For what children are not disciplined by their father? If you are not disciplined—and everyone undergoes discipline—then you are not legitimate, not true sons and daughters at all. Moreover, we have all had human fathers who disciplined us and we respected them for it. How much more should we submit to the Father of spirits and live! They disciplined us for a little while as they thought best; but God disciplines us for our good, in order that we may share in his holiness. No discipline seems pleasant at the time, but painful. Later on, however, it produces a harvest of righteousness and peace for those who have been trained by it. (Hebrews 12:7-11 NIV)*

Very early in life I realized that if I learned from other people's mistakes, I could avoid getting into trouble with my parents. When my brother or sister got punished, I observed what they had done wrong and determined not to do the same thing. This didn't protect me from making my own mistakes and erring in other ways, but it did set me on a lifelong course of making it a top priority to learn the easy way how to do what's right.

During my childhood, this earned me the reputation of being a "goodie-goodie" amongst my friends. Sometimes even "holier than thou" because I also prayed a lot and thought everyone should do likewise. It puzzled me why people used these nicknames as if they were insulting me. I didn't know it yet, but they were mocking the divine calling, which we all have, to become saints.

Somewhere along the way of maturing into an adult, avoiding the punishment of my dad grew into the desire to do only what God the Father wants me to do—"nothing more and nothing less" (as I say in my morning prayers)—even when it doesn't make sense or when it goes against my personal inclinations. My plan is to keep getting better and better at this (with the Holy Spirit's help).

"Do whatever he tells you" (from John 2:5) was the theme of a conference that Ralph and I attended in 1993. It beckoned us in giant letters painted across a wide banner above the stage. As we would later find out, this was the first clue that God was going to send us to Florida to become founders of Good News Ministries of Tampa Bay. But we had to go through a formation process—one that Abba himself designed.

The key skills of holy living are listening to, waiting for, and discovering God's Divine Will. This process requires a lot of time, the humility of self-doubt, plenty of mistakes and a desire to learn from our mistakes. Therefore, we should be forgiving and patient with ourselves when we err. Abba-Father is—but not forever; we all arrive at the day of reckoning when we discover that our unrepented sins have become "what you reap is what you sow":

> *Do not be deceived: God cannot be mocked. A man reaps what he sows. Whoever sows to please their flesh, from the flesh will reap destruction; whoever sows to please the Spirit, from the Spirit will reap eternal life (Galatians 6:7-8 NIV).*

Why is obedience so difficult at times? Why do we rebel? The answer lies in the question of what motivates our obedience: Is it the fear of punishment? Or is it a genuine love for God? If it's the fear of punishment, of course we want to rebel from that kind of Father! If it's love, we want to please our Father just like any child who wants to do good deeds for a parent out of sheer appreciation.

If it's love, our obedience is grounded in the confidence that God knows what's best for us. But do our decisions always show this confidence?

Every teaching of Jesus, every law that Jesus came to fulfill, every command that Jesus gave: These were not restrictions of our fun or free will. They were protections against evil.

> *But the righteous live forever, / and their reward is with the Lord; / the Most High takes care of them. / Therefore they will receive a glorious crown / and a beautiful diadem from the hand of the Lord, / because with his right hand he will cover them, / and with his arm he will shield them. (Wisdom 5:15-16 NRSV)*

The Father always has our best interests at heart. He only wants to bless us and to bless others through us. The teachings of Christ are an embrace by Abba-Father's love, and it is felt by those who want to be holy, that is, unless we've been made numb by the fear of punishment doled out from a Father upon whom we've projected human traits.

Have you thought that perhaps a disease you suffer from or the lack of healing despite many prayers is God's punishment for sin? Or that his disapproval was revealed through a car accident, or the fire that burned down the house, or the loss of a job, or any other hardship?

Terrible things happen merely because we are living on Earth instead of in Heaven, not because God is punishing us. But sometimes what we suffer is a reaping of what we've sown, like the knee pain caused by being overweight, or like the absence of friends caused by lying to them. In effect, we are punishing ourselves—and God permits this because he knows that good can come from it and he won't override our free will decisions even though he knows the consequences that we will face. This might sound unloving but wait till you see the good that comes from it!

The role of repentance in discipline

When we think of God as The Punisher, our natural inclination is to live in self-protection mode. We convince ourselves and others that what we're doing that *feels* wrong is really *not* wrong. To avoid punishment (or so we think), we choose to believe that sin is not sin—which is the heresy of moral relativism. When we sin, we justify ourselves, blame others for our mistakes, and hide from our need to repent.

The word "repent" usually carries with it the idea that we are bad, and so we prefer to believe that we are okay no matter what we've done. But "repent" actually means "to change direction" after realizing that where we've been going (or what we've been doing) is wrong.

In other words (and it's healing to know this), it's the direction we're headed in that's bad, not us.

God made each of us good! Yes, even you and even the worst person in the world. Holiness is our core nature, our true nature. On the sixth day of creation, God said, "Let us make humans next—*in our image, in our likeness.*" God's traits are at the core of our nature! He looked over everything he had created—including *you*—and declared it "very good." (See Genesis 1:26-31.)

Sin—*even when we don't believe it's a sin*—interrupts our goodness. It interrupts our relationship with our Good Father, so he sent Jesus the Savior to redirect us away from the path to Hell and toward the path to Heaven. Jesus took our sins upon his sinless self and nailed them to the Cross with his Body. He conquered sin for us by letting our sins destroy him, dying for us. Then he overcame this destruction through his resurrection. When we embrace this truth, we are set free to be who we really are (made in the image of our Father).

> *Therefore, there is now no condemnation for those who are in Christ Jesus, because through Christ Jesus the law of the Spirit*

who gives life has set you free from the law of sin and death. (Romans 8:1-2 NIV)

We are saints who still need a lot of purification, but we are not bad people. We are cherished children of a caring Father. "Those whom I love I rebuke and discipline," he says. "So be earnest and repent." (Revelation 3:19 NIV)

Most of us tend to think that the word "discipline" is a synonym for "punishment." But the discipline of Abba-Father is best described as "formation"—like a potter shaping a beautiful clay vase that will someday hold sweet-smelling flowers.

Indeed, we have sinned, "Yet you, LORD, are our Father. / We are the clay, you are the potter; / we are all the work of your hand." (Isaiah 64:8 NIV)

But the pot he was shaping from the clay was marred in his hands; so the potter formed it into another pot, shaping it as seemed best to him (Jeremiah 18:4 NIV).

Our Loving Father reshapes our lives in order to bring our best selves out from within.

There are three phases in the disciplinary process. First, marred by our own sins, we suffer the consequences of wrong decisions. For example, a man who is attached to the things of this world—his house, his car, his books, his plans—suffers greatly when he loses them. In this phase, it's all about what *we* want. We want the suffering to end, and our prayers are meant to convince God to fix things.

What God does, however, is hold in his hands our brokenness and all of our potential for what we could become. While he waits for us to surrender to his potter's wheel, he lets us continue to damage ourselves until we decide we are willing to enter the second phase.

Now it becomes all about what *God* wants. We seek the face of God. And he smiles as he accepts from us the gift of misshapen clay that came from our poor decisions, our woundedness, and our rebellions. Our prayers are meant to serve God.

This is when the man in our example decides that he really doesn't need all of his worldly stuff. More than anything else, he wants to have an intimate relationship with God as a personal friend and a caring Father. Now the Father is free to reshape the man's life into something more useful, something that looks different than before.

There is one more stage. The third stage is when the new life—the reshaped pot—benefits others. It becomes all about the sufferings of others and what we can do to help. Our prayers are meant to detach us from everything self-centered. We seek to be the hands and face of God. (We will cover this in more depth in a later chapter.)

The real meaning of discipline

My dad was the family disciplinarian. He often told us that Mom was the one who understood the psychology of children and he only understood that he was elected to mete out the punishment. "Wait till your father gets home" is the way many mothers get their kids to behave if she can't do it with reasoning and rewards (unless the father no longer lives in the home; we'll cover this later, too). And so, when my dad came through the front door ready to relax after a long day of work and he was greeted by the need to discipline children, you can guess why I formed an image of the Father as short-tempered, unhappy, and tired of his children's stupid disobedience.

We all learned as children that upsetting the Father usually results in punishment.

Indeed, God's discipline sometimes is very punishing—but not because God is quick-tempered and tired of our sinfulness. Scripture tells us, *"Return to the LORD your God, for he is gracious and merciful, slow to anger, and abounding in steadfast love; and he relents over disaster"* (Joel 2:13 ESV).

Discipline feels punishing due to our own attitude, not God's. How reluctant are we to change? Do we hate our broken lives yet continue in our old ways despite how miserable we feel? Or are we willing to learn what Abba-Father is teaching us through it?

The word "discipline" actually means "train" or "prepare by instruction" as in teaching one how to do a task or get something done. It comes from the Latin word *disciplina*, which means instruction or knowledge. It shares the same root as *discipulus* from which we get the word "disciple."

During the Middle English years (c. 1100-1500), the word "discipline" became associated with mortification by scourging yourself as penance for sins. It's a perversion of what discipline is meant to be. And it still lingers: Instead of feeling good that we have learned something through discipline, we feel guilty. We are not gracious and merciful to ourselves. Even after going to Confession and hearing Jesus say, through the priest, "Your sins are forgiven," we beat ourselves up for what we did wrong.

Abba as Potter does not smash the sinner to reshape him. That would be unloving. To appreciate the discipline of Abba-Father, we must first focus on his merciful love instead of seeing him as a chastiser who never forgets how we erred. This change in our thinking isn't easy because we've been trained to chastise ourselves. And it's not easy because we realize that God is all-knowing and therefore it's impossible for him to forget our sins. Right? Therefore, we should not forget about them either. Do you have a problem forgiving yourself? If so, this is probably why.

One day I asked God if he really could forget our sins after we've repented and reconciled with him in the Sacrament of Confession. He replied, "Do you remember being born?"

"No, of course not," I said.

"But you know you were born."

"Yes, of course."

"In the same way, I know all the ways you have sinned, but I do not remember any of it since you repented and asked for My forgiveness. I have not dealt with you according to your sins or repaid you according to your iniquities. For as high as the Heavens are above the Earth, so great is My loving devotion to you. As far as the east is from the west, that's how far I have removed your transgressions from you. As a father has compassion on his children, so I have compassion on you. For I know how I formed you. I remember that you are weak, like dust." (See Psalm 103:10-14.)

Before moving forward from here, let me interject a question that I'm often asked: "*How* do you have conversations like that with him? How do you get him to answer your questions like a human being would?" I used to ask others the same question.

Hearing Abba-Father conversationally comes from many years of clearing out my misconceptions about him while learning to trust him more and more. It comes from being "baptized in" or anointed by the Holy Spirit through the Catholic Charismatic Renewal, for this makes all the difference between trying to succeed on my own and receiving supernatural help.

It also comes from my imagination. I ask the Holy Spirit to anoint my imagination every time I do a visual meditation or ask God a question. Then I trust that my submissive willingness to learn the truth is all that the Father needs to reach my heart with his words. His voice has my permission to reach the ears of my soul.

And it comes from scriptures too. Notice that his answer to my question above came from Psalm 103. I don't have the Bible memorized; I merely have read it enough and listened to it proclaimed in Sunday and daily Mass for many years. The idea or principle of a scripture comes to mind, not the chapter and verse. Later, I research it and find the scriptures that help answer my question.

The whole conversation takes place, usually, over the course of days and sometimes months. At first, I hear the short answer in my heart or soul or imagination (whichever you want to call it). This begins a process of continued reflection about it. More is revealed through a book I'm reading, or a comment made by my husband or a friend, or a hawk flying by, or anything that God in his infinite creativity chooses.

As long as what we hear during prayer does not contradict the Bible or the teachings of the Catholic Church, we can trust that it is God's voice and not the Devil's.

But could it be our own inner voice? Might it be our own will—our own desires or expectations? The answer lies in this: Does it require us to be submissive to the Father's will? Is it free of self-defensiveness and self-justification? Are we willing to bend our will and have our minds changed? Does it cause an "aha!" moment of a wonderful revelation, which feels good even though we discover we had been wrong about something? If the answers to these questions are "yes," then we can trust that we're listening to God's voice and not our own.

When the conversation feels like I'm the clay and the Divine Potter is reshaping me into becoming more like him, I know I can trust what I'm hearing.

Anyone who has entered the first phase of disciplinary growth, as described earlier in this chapter, has jumped onto the potter's wheel. Proverbs 3:32 (NASB) says, *"For the devious are an abomination to the LORD; / But he is intimate with the upright."* The devious are those who don't seek God at all. They plot and plan everything without him; they decide for themselves what is sinful and what is not.

The upright are those who seek God and want to embrace Divine Will—even though they obey him imperfectly. Saintliness is not about avoiding all sins. It's about accepting the Father's discipline like the clay pot accepts the potter's hands. We want him to lovingly (and yes, gently) reshape our own will so that it looks more and more like his.

It's a lifelong purification. It's an intimacy with the Potter who can make wonderful and beautiful treasures out of broken pieces.

Hidden blessings

Every rebuke from Abba-Father is a blessing. We know that he does everything for our good, but do we fully believe it? Not usually. During hardships, we demand that he quickly bring a stop to everything that's painful. We seek his helping hand and, if we can't see it, we feel abandoned or punished.

In truth, he never abandons us. Even when we are unfaithful to God, he remains faithful to us because he cannot forsake himself. It's impossible for him to stop loving us. He is always good and can never do evil (see 2 Timothy 2:13).

> Saint John of the Cross explained it this way: "*God sustains every soul and dwells in it substantially, even though it be that of the greatest sinner in the world, and this union is natural. The supernatural union exists when God's will and the soul's will are in conformity. Therefore, the soul rests transformed in God through love.*"

A very common question raised by hardships is, "Why me? Why do I have to suffer this?" There's an old cliché that contributes to the pain of this: "There but for the grace of God go I." We think it when we see someone else suffer. I wish I could erase this saying from the planet! For me and for many others it implies that God did not give his grace to that person who is suffering. With this possibility in the back of our minds, we could easily conclude that when it's our turn to say, "Why me?" it's because God has withdrawn his grace from us.

Not so!

Let's change the cliché to: "By the grace of God, he/she can get through this. I wonder if I can help." And change the "Why me?" to: "By the grace of God, I can get through this. I look forward to finding out how he will help me."

Not everything bad that happens is a punishment. But all—*everything*—is used by our loving Abba-Father to teach us something. For example, the sins we commit become lessons that strengthen us to resist sin. *"Those whom I love I rebuke and discipline. So be earnest and repent"* (Revelation 3:19 NIV). We learn from the troubles we caused when we gave into temptations.

The second type of lesson comes after making wrong decisions. We seek God's guidance but interpret it incorrectly. This is not a sin; it's a mistake. But mistakes can be as destructive as sins. We hate to admit our mistakes as much as we hate to admit that we've sinned. *"Humble yourselves, therefore, under God's mighty hand, that he may lift you up in due time. Cast all your anxiety on him because he cares for you"* (1 Peter 5:6-7 NIV).

And the third kind of lesson comes from being hurt by the sins and mistakes of others. God protects us, but not always in the way we want. He makes us stronger and teaches us to love our enemies. *"I will make you a wall to this people, a fortified wall of bronze; they will fight against you but will not overcome you, for I am with you to rescue and save you"* (Jeremiah 15:20 NIV).

In each case, we benefit because we learn something valuable.

Today's Exercise:
Find the Mercy in God's Discipline

One day I requested the prayers of a man (I'll call him "Luke") whose ministry was to help Christians discover new levels of freedom in their faith journeys. I hoped he would become a prayer partner for my work in Good News Ministries. However, Luke did not understand the purpose of our prayer sessions. He treated me as if I personally needed the same kind of help that everyone else came to get. He used a prayer formula he had learned and blamed me for the lack of results.

When our one-hour session timed out, I left feeling cut off, unserved, and unheard. Frustrated and hurt, the little girl in me who had felt unheard by her daddy wanted to cry. Before starting my car to drive home, I turned to Abba. "Bless what just happened, Father. Make good come from it. What do you want me to learn from it?"

Was Luke right about anything that I had rejected during our meeting? "No," he answered. But there were three lessons to learn.

One: I had committed the sin of arrogance. I had not humbled myself before the Lord to ask whether or not I should even go to Luke in the first place. Lesson learned: Remember to pray about every decision, even ones that seem obvious; God knows far more than I do about it.

Two: I had made a wrong assumption about Luke. Lesson learned: See the first lesson above.

Three: Luke was doing a ministry that requires supernatural faith. By that I mean relying on the gifts of the Holy Spirit that come from what many call the "Baptism of the Spirit." During our session, his comments seemed to lack the inspiration of the Holy Spirit. He followed a formula. At first, I dismissed this as just my imagination, hoping to be wrong. After all, Luke supposedly knew what to do. And I was determined to find the help that I had requested.

Lesson learned: Look for the personal relationship with the Holy Spirit others have before getting involved with them in ministry. The more inspired by the Spirit they are, the freer I can be with them and the more I'll be able to accomplish with them.

Abba-Father disciplined me well. I did not feel condemned by him. I felt stronger. It would take me a while before I could fully forgive Luke because the little girl in me cried about his disappointing and surprising lack of hearing me and understanding my needs.

When bad things happen to you, remember that you are being trained and reshaped, like an athlete in training. Ask yourself: How is the experience making me stronger?

Next, ask where the mercy is. Abba-Father's discipline always—definitely *always*—includes mercy. If we think we're being punished unmercifully, we're believing a lie that Satan is using to make us feel miserable and to falsify the image of God's Fatherhood. It's the Devil, not God, who punishes his victims unmercifully.

When we look for and identify where God's mercy is making good come from bad, we find the smiling face of our dear Abba-Father.

What is troubling you most right now? Describe it in a sentence or two below. Then make a list of what you have learned from this trouble so far. How is it making you stronger? How is God reshaping you?

_____
_____
_____
_____
_____
_____
_____
_____
_____
_____

10

Abba's Hidden Love in Our Confusion

When we try hard to discern God's will and then proceed with what we perceive as his guidance only to meet with failure, we understandably get lost in confusion. We wonder: "What happened? Why didn't this work out? I was following God. I was trusting God. And he led me into disaster! But this is not God's nature; perhaps I'm projecting onto him what a human has done to misguide me. Or is it my fault? Did I misinterpret his guidance?" More confusion.

"For I know the plans I have for you," declares the Lord,
"plans to prosper you and not to harm you, plans to give you
hope and a future. (Jeremiah 29:11 NIV)

In an earlier chapter, I shared the story of how Ralph and I built our house despite many obstacles. But there was one more coming straight at us—one that was both unexpected and devastating. It hit us just days before the closing date for the new house, just a couple of days before moving in. Ralph got laid off from work.

"Huh? How could that happen?" we wondered. "Where was God's protection? I don't understand. The timing couldn't be worse."

The bank's loan officer asked for proof of Ralph's employment right *after* he lost the job. God could have made him ask beforehand, so why didn't he? Instead, the loan officer found out about the loss of income. The bank would not grant us a mortgage. We were going to be stuck with a big construction loan and no house for it.

It looked like Father God was standing in the doorway of our new house, arms crossed, like a big, bully bouncer at a night club, telling us, "No, you can't get in." And it felt like God was towering over Ralph saying, "No, you can't have this job anymore." And there was no changing his mind. No way for Ralph to get his job back, no way to find a new job in time to save the house.

Sometimes we misinterpret the sternness of the Father as meanness. Like he's a bully and he's scowling at us no matter how well we behave. This happens because, when we were children, our human parents seemed very mean to us when in firm sternness they rightfully disciplined us. In truth, Abba-Father's sternness comes from his authority, and, like any king, what he says from his position of authority is what matters. It is not open for debate.

However, it's also true that Abba-Father, unlike many human parents, actually delights in us when we question him. This is appropriate in a healthy father-child relationship as long as the child is not questioning his authority but genuinely wants to learn and the parent has time and patience for it.

Abba-Father is always watching out for us, always planning what is good for us. It is much more beneficial for us that he applies his kingly authority for our sake, in the implementation of his plans, than it is to have to manage things on our own. If this is what we really want, then we'll discover the secret to living in the joy and peace of being under God's authority. It's as simple as one, two, three:

1. We give Father God the benefit of the doubt.
2. We choose to trust him.
3. And then we relax knowing that he's got everything under control even when things look chaotic.

As Ralph and I faced the huge losses of good employment and the house we had just finished building, we turned to God in prayer, still reeling from shock. The prayer was short and straight from the heart: "Help! What do we do now?"

Our Good Father did not delay his response. He told me, "Ralph's lay-off is an answer to your many prayers begging me to free him from the huge stress of working for that company."

My reply: "So, this is my fault then?"

I thought about my daily prayers spanning several years, asking for Ralph to be delivered from the job that made him miserable. "But now, Lord? You chose *now* to set him free from this suffering? I had expected You to help him find a replacement job. It would be much better, You know, to move him from one job to the next without a gap in time and income."

Of course, God did know that—and more, much more about the situation. For reasons we would only later find out, it was better for Ralph to retire early. But it was too soon to know this. The confusion continued.

God also knew that there was no need to panic. The loan officer called back and asked about *my* income. It was, when combined with Ralph's retirement 401k fund, enough to grant us the mortgage. We'd have to cut back on other expenses, but we could afford to keep the house.

Our new prayer became: "Dear Lord, help Ralph find a new job before his severance package runs out." God answered this prayer even though he knew that it would be better for Ralph to retire now. The new job started exactly when the severance package ended. God's perfect timing (though we had wanted it sooner).

And then, two years later, he was laid off from this company too. And thus began his early retirement, which enabled him to help me with the responsibilities of caring for my elderly parents. Soon after, a checkup with the doctor revealed a problem with his heart. The stresses of working in the fast-paced corporate world could have killed him.

The origins of our confusion

Felisha felt very confused when God's guidance led her to a job she didn't get.

"I had what I thought was an excellent opportunity," she says, "for a full-time job with many perks. The greatest perk would have been that my husband and I could live together all the time instead of only on weekends. I did not want the job, but it was a good opportunity, so I discussed it with my husband, and I took it before the Lord."

She waited on the Lord and prayed and sought his will. "During my prayer times, I received many confirmations from the Word of God assuring me that the battle was the Lord's, etc. My trust and faith in God were at the highest point. I did my best to prepare for the exam that was required to get the job. I took it very seriously, trusting that God would make the impossible possible."

When it came time for the test, "I failed miserably. Even though I was the *only* candidate who sat for the exam, I did not get the job. Since then, I don't know how to discern God's will for me. My prayer life has really suffered, and I feel horribly let down by God. When I think about trusting him, I tell myself, 'Don't be too sure that he's going to keep his word.' A horrible experience! It was such an ordeal and so humiliating."

Often, confusion originates with the idea that we have understood his guidance correctly, when in fact we did not. Listen to the example of Jeannette and Gerald's story:

Jeannette shares, "After living in one city for 27 years, my husband and I decided he would take a promotion within the company he worked for, although it would require him to move to another city. The good points were that we were going to be empty nesters in two years, and we looked forward to new adventures in a different area, plus my husband would have a new challenge for several years before he retired, plus one of the places he would travel to was our hometown where both of our aging parents still lived. All of these things sounded good to us."

In trying to discern God's will, she says, "We talked to our youngest son who was a sophomore in high school. Since he had lived here his entire life, had long-time classmates and friends, and was on the basketball team at school, if he vehemently objected, we would not make the move. As it turned out, he thought it would be exciting to meet new friends and get onto one of the five basketball teams of this new and larger parochial high school. So, my husband accepted the job and we made plans to move. We put our home on the market and house-hunted in the new city. When spring arrived, my son was treated to a going away party by his basketball team."

Then came the confusion. "Our home was not selling, and I could not find one in the new city that met our criteria. There had been one possibility: We found a builder who had a lot that we liked. But as time passed, the lot was sold to someone else. Then, in addition to the housing situation not working out in a timely manner, we needed to pay a large non-refundable deposit to the parochial high school that my son would attend for his junior year."

Not knowing what else to do, Gerald asked his company if he could accept the new position right away but delay moving for two years until their son would graduate from high school. They agreed.

Jeannette says, "In light of these disharmonious things, we asked God for clarity as to how we should proceed. We finally told God that if our home sold before the school deposit was due, we'd put the deposit down in the new city, taking the sale of our house as a "go-ahead" sign from him. If it did not sell, we would stay back for two years and let our son graduate from his current high school. As it turned out, our home did not sell. We told our son about the situation. His reaction was a bit of a surprise to us. He was glad that we would not be moving. He said he got to thinking about how he'd miss his friends and everything else in his current situation. However, he did not tell us because he did not want to ruin his dad's opportunity. Now he was glad of our change of plans and looked forward to staying put."

Eventually the realtor that Jeannette and Gerald had used in the new city called to report that the builder's lot they had liked so much had become available. The person who was going to build on it had a job change and could no longer do it.

"Are you interested?" the realtor asked. The only problem she saw with it was that it would take about a year to build the house after everything was approved. Jeannette and Gerard were pleased; this was not a problem at all. They saw it as God's timing and thanked him. As it turned out, there were "snags" along the way that delayed the building process, and the house was not completed until their son went off to college. God's perfect timing had guided the plan and he protected Jeannette and Gerard from making a mistake even while they were unaware of his help.

Often our confusion comes from projecting our own assumptions or hopes into whatever God is trying to say and do. This happens to me. My thoughts are rich with ideas, and if I don't hear Abba-Father fast enough or clearly enough, my brain fills in the blanks.

To counter this, I have found this Increase/Decrease prayer to be very helpful: *"Abba-Father, renew me in your Holy Spirit. Holy Spirit, increase in me the desire and energy to do ____ if it is the Father's Divine Will. If it is not Your will, or not at this time, then whenever I think about proceeding with it, drain me of energy and decrease in me the desire to do it."* After that, I have to pay attention to my energy level.

Here's a true example of how this works: Before starting this book, the Increase/Decrease prayer increased my energy, the flow of ideas, and my desire to write it so much that eventually the book overtook my busy schedule. I just had to take time off for it.

On other occasions, when I begin to implement a plan and I feel lethargic about it, my first inclination is to force myself to do it anyway just to get it done—in the name of self-discipline. But this, I've learned, is usually the wrong response. I need to trust the lack of energy as an answer to the Increase/Decrease prayer.

A lack of energy could have other causes, too. As a fail-safe measure, I ask Abba-Father to give me a divine push in the right direction if I'm misunderstanding his guidance.

We also need to consider that our Enemy might be interfering. When I began editing the final draft of this book, I lost all energy and inspiration for chapter two. So, I prayed the Increase/Decrease prayer, but that did not work. Finally, I tried some spiritual warfare prayers. I sent "any demons who are interfering" to the foot of the Cross of Jesus to be covered by his blood. That worked! The energy and inspiration began to flow again.

(Note: Do not attempt to handle demons without proper training, except for using the basic tools that Jesus has given us through the Church, such as holy water, the Rosary, and repeating the name of Jesus out loud.)

Why does God allow us to get confused?

God blesses our confusions. It's part of the humbling process of realizing that our understanding of God's guidance is tainted by the limitations of our perceptions. Confusion is a sign that we're getting mixed messages and we cannot sort out which is the Father's voice. Not until we repent of choosing for ourselves what we think God "should" do. And perhaps we also need to repent of other sins because our sins give the Devil permission to confuse us.

Our confusion is worsened by:

- The half-truth messages of fear. (For example, "What if I don't get a new job? We'll end up losing our house!") The cure: Ask the Holy Spirit to help you identify the lie that the fear is telling you so that you can realize the opposite, the truth that the Father is revealing.
- Resentment toward people who contributed to the problem. ("I got laid off because the manager above me was prejudiced against me. It's his fault.") The cure: Forgive them.
- Anger because we did not get what we wanted. Mix this with pride and it's a very hard confusion to overcome. The cure: Forgive God and accept responsibility for misinterpreting his guidance or, when appropriate, choose to persevere until his full plan is viewable in hindsight.

This is why we should not try to discern God's will on our own. God values one-on-one interaction with us, but he also wants to clarify and confirm his plans through others. A spiritual director, counselor, or a community of Christ-centered, Spirit-filled friends can help us get pointed in the right direction when we need the extra help—especially when our personal prayer time does not bring clarity and we need to make a decision without further delay, or when we make every effort to discern God's will correctly and we still remain confused.

Even while we are in a state of confusion, we can relax in the security of knowing that Abba-Father is with us and cares very much about us. It helps to remember that God will make good come from everything—including confusion. The question is not: "Why is God confusing me?" Rather, the true question is: "What does God want me to learn from this?" Confusion turns into peaceful joy when we discover the answer to this one.

Think of confusion as a grey fog covering the path that you're traveling. You're on the right path, but you can't see how everything is already in place ahead of you, right where they need to be. The fog hides the trees and flowers that make the journey beautiful. It hides the cottage that the Father has provided for shelter. It hides the destination that he wants you to reach. They are all just beyond your view.

Nor can you see the fork in the road. You've asked for Abba's protection from wrong decisions. Therefore, he's directing your feet in the right direction, and although the left side of the fork is where you think you should be headed, he's got you going up the right side of the fork. Something about this doesn't seem right, and the fog makes this feeling turn scary. But really it is very good!

Then you crash into a hard wall. You didn't see yourself headed toward it. It's God's protection preventing you from going the wrong way! However, this might not become visible to you until later, when you can look back.

In the journey of following Abba-Father through the fog of confusion, we are being tested and tried. The test is for our benefit. We learn from it just how much our trust in the Father has grown (or not).

I often joke, "God, you duped me, and I allowed myself to be duped."

God "duped" me into wanting a priest-friend to become the first chaplain of Good News Ministries. We later discovered that alcoholism was handicapping him emotionally and in his ministry. Both of his parents had been alcoholics, and he had become an alcoholic himself. Abba-Father knew that we would never have invited him to move to Florida if, during our 20 years of prior friendship, we had discovered his alcoholism and understood the effects of codependency. Abba-Father also knew how much more effective in helping others I would become after learning how to deal with our friend's problems.

I could also say that Abba-Father "duped" us into moving from New Jersey to Florida in order to start this ministry in 1995. We had no idea about this plan. We thought we were moving just to get away from snow and high taxes. It was a good "duping," but it changed our lives in more ways than we had been able to predict.

In 1994, Ralph and I had served on the core team of a different Good News Ministries. The New Jersey group planned a week-long evangelization school for our parish, to be held in November. To our surprise, we never got to be part of that great event. Instead, God inspired our family to move to Florida. This was very confusing.

The Holy Spirit energized us with a desire to move. At first, we tried to find a new house in the same town. We envisioned staying in our beloved parish and continuing with the New Jersey School of Evangelization. Remember what I said earlier about God being a good Father who protects us from going in wrong directions? There were many forks in the fog-filled path that he put us on. It was all very confusing, but gradually the inexplicable desire to sell our house pushed us farther and farther south until we landed in Florida.

On January 30, 1995, we found ourselves in a restaurant near our new home, standing in front of Charlie Osburn, the man who had trained the New Jersey team. He had come here to give a seminar. (Was this timing and location just a coincidence?) Recognizing us, he pointed out to us a core team that the Lord had already put together for a Good News Ministries of Tampa Bay. The new ministry was still only a dream and a prayer for these people. They had been praying the Rosary for two years asking God to provide leaders.

Charlie asked, "Will you be those leaders?" We said yes and questioned our sanity because we had seen the work that goes into this.

Our Wise Father knew that we would have said "no" if Charlie had invited us to start Good News Ministries of Tampa Bay while we still lived in New Jersey.

God often confirms his guidance through circumstances. Be on the alert! When situations happen outside of your control, God is planning something good that seems (at first) very confusing. Ride it out. Keep praying. Trust your Wise Father. Even if the Devil is behind the confusing, God is allowing it so that he can humiliate the Devil by raising you up in an awesome, better-than-expected plan.

As Gift Nyirenda says, "We prefer to control our destiny, forgetting God's role and hand in all of this. God never has a plan of fear, pain, and suffering for us. Jesus Christ took it all on the Cross then opened a way for us to reconcile ourselves to God through an advocate, the Holy Spirit. When the Holy Spirit speaks to us, all we need to do is cooperate."

Today's Exercise:
Journey from confusion to blessings

We gain new spiritual strength only through a process that at times is too confusing to understand. This growth happens not by God making everything easy but by us responding to God's invitation to walk through the difficulties with him. We need to remember this when we want to run away from the confusion or away from God for apparently causing the confusion. Our Good Father wants us to walk with him through the grey fog all the way to the blessings that he knows are waiting for us. He's inviting us to a more intimate Father-child relationship.

Saint Theodora Guerin knew this. She said, "The way is not yet clear. Grope along slowly. Do not press matters; be patient, be trustful. With Jesus, what shall we have to fear?" As you meditate on this, remember that Jesus takes us to the Father. Jesus reveals the Father to us. So, we can rightfully say, "With the Father, what shall I have to fear?"

To us, the fog looks like a curse; a hardship to get rid of. But to our Good Father, it's an adventure of journeying hand-in-hand. He sees what's ahead. He wants to make sure that we don't miss it! Think of him like a treasure hunter who has memorized the treasure map. Just keep clinging to his hand. Keep going. With Abba-Father at your side, you'll reach the treasures that he's very eager to give you.

The Bible shows countless evidence that God rejoices in this Father-child partnership. The prophet Elisha required Naaman to wash himself seven times in the Jordan River to be healed of leprosy. (See 2 Kings 5.) The idea confused Naaman so much that he almost didn't do it. He had expected Elisha to call upon his God, wave his hand, and provide an instant cure. When he didn't get what he expected, he got hot-headed and angry. Fortunately, his servants convinced him to give it a try. (They were the community God spoke through to get Naaman pointed in the right direction when he needed the extra help.) After he accepted his own part in the plan and cooperated with the instructions, he received his healing.

It's not as if Elisha wasn't able to provide an instant healing. In 2 Kings 6, he said one short prayer and all the soldiers of the enemy were blinded (verse 18). Later, he said another short prayer and they were all instantly healed (verse 20).

Why then did God, through Elisha, want Naaman to journey through confusion before reaching his cure?

In John 9:1-7, Jesus healed a blind man by spitting on the ground and making a mud paste with his saliva. I'll bet this man was confused by this at least just a little, huh? Jesus applied the mud to the man's eyes and then instructed him to wash it off in the Pool of Siloam. Only after complying with Jesus' strange way of dealing with it did he receive his healing.

At other times, Jesus healed people with only a word or a gesture. Why did Jesus give this particular man something to do first? Because the Father had a special plan for him. The Bible does not give us the follow-up story; we can only guess at what God had in mind for him. Perhaps this very intimate encounter with Jesus set him on the path of becoming an evangelizer who could heal people's hearts when they were doubting that God truly cares.

Abba-Father has gifted us with freedom, intelligence, and creativity to participate in what he is doing. He enjoys involving us in the process. At first, we might suffer the uncertainty of traveling blindly on a fog-filled road. But it's not because God delights in confusing us. It's because there's something to learn from it and he's giving us the opportunity to discover it.

We learn more from mistakes than from easy successes.

In big problems, look for small blessings. Eventually you'll be able to see huge blessings, but until then, look for the small clues about the Father's helpful involvement. This will sustain you by bringing you relief and encouragement. Small blessings are seeds that Abba-Father has planted. Cultivate them.

Instead of focusing on what didn't go right, take a deep breath, and forgive God or yourself or whomever has triggered anger, frustration, or doubt. And then ask the Holy Spirit to help you notice and identify any good that has come from the journey of walking through the trial. Be sure to look carefully enough to see the smallest of blessings. Small things often float past us like dust in the air around us, capturing our attention only when the light hits the particles from just the right angle.

What blessings can you identify from the confusing problem that has been on your mind while reading this chapter? Write them down.

_____

_____

_____

_____

_____
_____
_____
_____
_____
_____
_____
_____

Every one of these blessings is a seed that Abba-Father has planted for you. They will sprout and grow from the attention you give to them. Protect these seeds by looking at what you wrote today, and add more to the list as the days go by. Enrich the soil of your spiritual life by feeding your soul (for example, by daily Mass, monthly Confession, meditating on scriptures, studying Church teachings, listening to and singing along with praise and worship music, etc.)

Thus, these small blessings will grow and gain strength. They will change the landscape of your life. In fact, the trial that was so frustrating will eventually evolve. The fog of confusion will lift. Although the journey might be long, you'll finally see a scenario or a solution that's better than what you had ever envisioned.

When Dawn retired from a career of 34 years in education, she was not ready to quit being a teacher. "I was still too young to retire," she says about the confusion she felt. "But after a year of retirement, God put me in a place that was a blessing—working in a Catholic school. I love my second career! Don't get me wrong, I loved my first career and cared for my students, but things had started to become a job, not fun or rewarding. I never expected to be where I am today. God knew all along that I would be blessed, happy, and able to grow spiritually here. I will be forever grateful that he heard my disappointment about retiring and granted me the job I currently have."

The cure for confusion

Abba-Father does not enjoy putting us through the torments of confusion. He gave us a way out—for example, in Acts 1:7-8 (NIV). When Jesus was ready to ascend to Heaven, his disciples questioned him, trying to clear up their confusion about God's plans. They asked him, "Lord, are you going to restore the kingdom to Israel now?"

He replied: "It is not for you to know the times or dates the Father has set by his own authority. But you will receive power when the Holy Spirit comes on you."

Abba-Father's authority is key here. We need to trust it. He doesn't always clear up our confusion, but he does always make clear his presence and his involvement. But we can only see it if we seek it.

More important than knowing what to expect is to know that *God* knows. One of my favorite mottos is: "I don't know what the future holds, but I know Who holds the future."

God gives us whatever we need for doing our best and enjoying this earthly life in the most beneficial way. When we are confused, when we have unanswered questions, the Holy Spirit is our aid and our ally. The Holy Spirit is the divine authority of God activating his helpfulness in our journey of becoming more and more like Christ.

Jesus said that the Holy Spirit will teach us everything we need to know (see John 14:26). This does not mean that we become all-knowing; it means that we can trust the all-knowingness of God and safely believe that he will teach us what we need to know when we need to know it. His knowledge will assist us. And if it seems like he's not helping us, it means that we can ask the Holy Spirit to help us understand how we are projecting onto the Father some human traits that seem to limit his help.

What if we find ourselves in a failure or in a troubling situation after trying to discern and follow God's will? If we tried our best, we need to forgive ourselves and trust God: The journey is not over yet. And if the failure comes from our sinful decisions, we need to go to the Sacrament of Confession to receive God's forgiveness too.

Examining where we went wrong can increase our confusion—at first. In truth, this is the path to peaceful joy. Instead of feeling bad about getting it wrong, we need to remind ourselves that, for as long as we live on Earth, we're imperfect interpreters of God's will—and this is okay! God does not hold it against us. So, why should we? What really matters is that we try our best. And each day, our best becomes a little better than it was the day before. The Father is delighted with every little step we take in our wobbly walk closer to the innermost depths of his heart.

With God on our side, confusion is simply a temporary fog. We can peacefully wait for the Holy Spirit to teach us what we need to know at the time we need to know it. It rarely comes sooner because our Good Father is teaching us to trust him more.

If we don't take this introspective route, confusion can become a tactic of the enemy. Paul told the Galatians:

> *"I am astonished that you are so quickly deserting the one who called you to live in the grace of Christ and are turning to a different gospel—which is really no gospel at all. Evidently some people are throwing you into confusion and are trying to pervert the gospel of Christ."* (Galatians 1:6-7 NIV)

Merry was born in Indonesia but, due to racism, she never liked being Indonesian. She says, "When I stayed in Australia for seven years, I loved every minute of it. I felt more at home there than I did back in Indonesia." Then she fell in love with an Indonesian man. She describes how this caused confusion, which later led to many blessings: "The man I was about to marry needed to reside in Indonesia in order to continue his father's business. Also, because he is the only son, his parents hoped he would take care of them in their old age."

She continues: "Against all of my family's advice, I decided to move back to Indonesia, the country I disliked. I gave up the bright future for my career and decided to help my new husband with his factory." She chose love above her own wants.

"Well, things have not turned out as well as I expected," she says. "During very difficult times, I have wondered if I made a mistake going back to Indonesia. Especially when I saw that all of my sisters in Australia are able to afford houses and cars while I am trying to save this struggling business."

However, when she turned away from the sources of her confusion to find out what Abba-Father was doing, she realized that God has been blessing her with more important things, which money cannot buy. "I was blessed with two children, and through loving them and forgiving them, I learned so much from them. At the beginning, I thought children were a burden: more financial responsibility and more moral responsibility teaching them good human values. But now I often realize that the children are teaching me lots of wisdom. I've learned from them how to live in the now. I've learned from them how to forgive by seeing how they forgive me even after I was verbally mean to them. In loving them, I feel as if I am giving myself the love that I didn't have much of during childhood. I have become a much better person because of them."

Merry has described multiple big blessings. But that's not all! She reports, "Being in Indonesia also means that I get to be closer to my parents. I didn't have good relationships with them, but watching them try to love my difficult brother, I can forgive them for what they have done or have not done to me, because I can see that they have love. They just don't know how to express their love because they didn't receive much love from their parents either."

And there's more. Merry says, "Spiritually I feel that, by being put into very difficult and humbling situations, I learned to see things from the 'poor beggar' point of view instead of judging people for not being as good as I assumed they should be."

Then she notes, "I believe that I wouldn't have learned so much if I had stayed in Australia and lived my own carefree life."

Chapter 10: Abba's Hidden Love in Our Confusion

Every day there is something to be confused about. Remember that confusion isn't evidence that God doesn't care. Or that God cares but we're too blind to see it. It's just an opportunity. Our Good Father always wants confusion to become a source of new blessings.

When anxiety, fear, and anger about the uncertainties of God's guidance hide the blessings, it's time to stop what we're doing and sit still with the Lord. I've found that the best place for this is in church during Mass or during Adoration of the Blessed Sacrament. Here is where we are most closely connected to God. The Holy Spirit has greater access to our thought processes. It's a place where we put our focus on Jesus, which removes our focus from the grey fog of confusion and the dark elements in it that frighten us.

Clarity arises from this change of focus. Even in the continued unknowing of a challenging situation, we more clearly understand that Abba-Father is watching out for us. He is taking good care of us. He is forging for us a future that will resemble what we had feared but which will soon produce special blessings that we cannot yet imagine. Rather than dread the future we fear, we can look for the blessings. Every little blessing is evidence that a very big blessing is waiting for us. Rejoice in this truth. Give God your thanks for it now; don't wait until the fog clears. This exchange of love will lift your spirits. And then this, too, will become one of the blessings you get to enjoy.

To conclude Workbook #1 in the three-part series on The Father's Heart, write a prayer thanking Abba Father for the blessings you named earlier in this chapter.

_____
_____
_____
_____
_____
_____
_____
_____
_____
_____
_____
_____
_____

Congratulations! You are not the same as you were when you first picked up this book. To continue your healing journey into the Father's Heart, be sure to get books 2 and 3:

Love that Heals Your Deepest Longing
The Victory of God's Fatherhood

www.ingramcontent.com/pod-product-compliance
Lightning Source LLC
LaVergne TN
LVHW020927090426
835512LV00020B/3245